Locke

on Human Understanding

This Routledge Philosophy GuideBook introduces John Locke and his major work, *An Essay Concerning Human Understanding*. Locke's *Essay* remains a key work in a number of fields of philosophy, notably in epistemology, metaphysics and the philosophies of mind and language. It is also a key text in courses on modern philosophy – where Locke is often studied (increasingly controversially) as the first of the British Empiricists. Knowledge of the text is vital for any student of philosophy.

Jonathan Lowe's approach enables students to study Locke's *Essay* effectively. Locke's life and works are placed in their historical context to help the student understand the importance of the *Essay* in his time. Lowe then provides a critical examination of the leading themes in the *Essay*, drawing out the main lines of Locke's thinking on innate ideas, perception, primary and secondary qualities, substance, personal identity, free will and action, language, and knowledge. He considers important recent work on Locke and shows this great English philosopher's continuing importance in modern philosophical thought.

Locke on Human Understanding is ideal for students studying Locke for the first time and provides essential background for the many areas of philosophy in which the *Essay* has proved to be so influential. Locke's important work in political philosophy will be considered in a separate GuideBook, *Locke on Government*.

E. J. Lowe is Reader in Philosophy at the University of Durham. He is the author of *Kinds of Being* (1989).

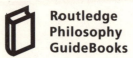

Routledge Philosophy GuideBooks

Edited by Tim Crane and Jonathan Wolff
University College London

Plato and the *Republic*
Nickolas Pappas

Locke on Government
D. A. Lloyd Thomas

London and New York

Routledge Philosophy GuideBook to

Locke

on

Human

Understanding

■ E. J. Lowe

ROUTLEDGE

First published 1995
by Routledge
11 New Fetter Lane,
London EC4P 4EE

Simultaneously published in the
USA and Canada
by Routledge
29 West 35th Street.
New York NY 10001

*Routledge is an imprint of the
Taylor & Francis Group*

© 1995 E. J. Lowe

Reprinted 1999

Text design: Barker/Hilsdon

Typeset in Times and Frutiger by
Florencetype Ltd, Stoodleigh, Devon

Printed and bound in Great Britain by
TJ International Ltd, Padstow, Cornwall

*British Library Cataloguing in
Publication Data*

A catalogue record for this book is
available from the British Library

*Library of Congress Cataloging in
Publication Data*

Lowe, E. J. (E. Jonathan)
Locke on human understanding / E.
J. Lowe.
p. cm. — (Routledge philosophy
guidebooks)
Includes bibliographical references
(p.) and index.

ISBN 0-415-10090-9 : $45.00
(U.S.). — ISBN 0-415-10091-7 :
$12.95 (U.S.)

1. Locke, John, 1632–1704.—Essay
concerning human understanding.
2. Knowledge, Theory. I. Title. II.
Series: Routledge Philosophy
GuideBooks.
B1294.L65 1995
121—dc20   94-43131
                              CIP

ISBN 0–415–10090–9 (hbk)
ISBN 0–415–10091–7 (pbk)

Contents

Preface

In this book I present a critical examination of leading themes in John Locke's *Essay Concerning Human Understanding*, with a view to situating Locke's ideas within the broader context of intellectual history and assessing their relevance to modern philosophical thought. In general my treatment is sympathetic to Locke's approach to many issues, while disagreeing with him on matters of detail. I maintain that Locke has greater relevance to modern thought than almost any other leading philosopher of his time.

In my exposition of Locke's views, I take into account some important recent developments in Locke scholarship, but I am more concerned to present and defend my own account of his views than to criticise the accounts of others. Where appropriate, scholarly disagreements are registered and discussed, but not at the expense of obscuring the main lines of Locke's thinking. Each chapter of the book, after providing a critical examination of Locke's position, proposes and defends a particular solution to the problems with which he was grappling – a solution which is often broadly sympathetic to Locke's own approach.

This book differs from other recent studies of Locke in several ways, notably in its exclusive focus on the *Essay*, in its selection of themes for discussion (such as the topic of action, which is often neglected), and perhaps above all in its defence of certain Lockean views which are still unfashionable (for example, on perception, action and language). The book presupposes no prior knowledge of Locke's work and only a basic grounding in philosophy.

The topics from the *Essay* which I have chosen to examine are ones which, in my estimation, have contributed most to its lasting influence as a work of philosophy, and the order in which I deal with them corresponds very closely to that in which they appear in the *Essay*. Chapter 2 focuses on Book I of the *Essay* ('Of Innate Notions'), Chapters 3 to 6 on Book II ('Of Ideas'), Chapter 7 on Book III ('Of Words') and Chapter 8 on Book IV ('Of Knowledge and Opinion'). Chapter 6, on Locke's theory of action, is placed after an examination of his views on substance and identity – contrary to the order of these topics in the *Essay* itself – because I think it is helpful to be aware of Locke's views about persons and personal identity before discussing his conception of personal agency.

Passages from the *Essay* quoted within the text are taken from Peter H. Nidditch's now standard Clarendon Edition of 1975, and their location in the *Essay* is indicated in the following fashion: '2.8.13' means 'Book II, Chapter VIII, Section 13 of the *Essay*'.

I am most grateful to Jonathan Wolff and to an anonymous referee for their helpful comments on earlier drafts of this book.

E. J. LOWE

July 1994

Chapter 1

Introduction: Locke's life and work

[handwritten margin notes: inculcation of political theory with religious values]

[handwritten margin notes: severe treatment at Westminster school]

[handwritten margin note: protestantism]

[handwritten margin notes: humane education (i.e. 'Emile')]

Locke's life and times

John Locke lived during a particularly turbulent period of English history and was personally associated with some of its most dramatic episodes, despite possessing a rather quiet and retiring character. He was born in Somerset in 1632, the son of a small landowner and attorney, also named John (1606–61), and his wife Agnes (1597–1654). In spite of these relatively humble beginnings, he received an excellent education, first at Westminster School and then at Christ Church, Oxford. These advantages were made possible through connections which his father had with people richer and more influential than himself. Patronage of this sort was one of the few means available in seventeenth-century England for people of little wealth to advance themselves, and Locke was to rely on it for a good deal of his life, ultimately rising to positions of considerable importance. Perhaps the most lasting legacy that Locke received from his parents, however, was his strong

Protestant faith, which was to exercise a very large influence on his future intellectual development and political allegiances.

After receiving his B.A. degree at Oxford University in 1656, following a traditional course of study in Arts, Locke held on to his studentship at Christ Church, entitling him to rooms in college and a stipend – a position which he retained until he was expelled at the direct instigation of Charles II (1630–85) in 1684, as a consequence of Locke's involvement with political groupings opposed to royal policies at the time. At Oxford, Locke was engaged not only in philosophical and theological studies, but was also particularly interested in medicine, and indeed in science quite generally (he became a fellow of the recently founded Royal Society in 1668). Locke's interest in medicine was fostered by his association with the eminent physician Thomas Sydenham (1624–89), and he was eventually to receive the medical degree of M.B. from Oxford University in 1675. His knowledge of medicine was to stand him in good stead when, after a chance meeting in 1666 with Lord Ashley (1621–83), then the Chancellor of the Exchequer, he became Lord Ashley's medical adviser, taking up residence in his London house in 1667 and staying there until 1675. Locke was responsible for overseeing a serious liver operation on Lord Ashley in 1668, from which the patient recovered, thereafter regarding Locke as one of his closest friends and confidants.

Locke's association with Lord Ashley – soon to become the first Earl of Shaftesbury (1672) – was the most momentous development in his career. Shaftesbury's influence at the court of Charles II was very great until the king dismissed him in 1673, though he was briefly to return to public office in 1679. From this time onwards English politics were greatly disturbed by the problem of the succession to the throne, Charles II having no children and his brother and heir, James II (1633–1707), being known for his strong allegiance to Roman Catholicism. Whig politicians like Ashley and his circle, which included Locke in a minor capacity, wanted a bill to be passed by Parliament excluding James from the succession – a move very much opposed by Charles II and his court. At this time royal power was still very considerable, and opposition like Shaftesbury's extremely dangerous. Shaftesbury himself escaped to the Netherlands in 1682 after a charge of treason had been levelled against him, but died soon after his arrival, early in 1683.

By this time Locke, who had been travelling abroad during 1675–9 but had not resumed his membership of Shaftesbury's household upon his return, was still closely associated with Shaftesbury's circle and hence in considerable personal danger himself. Government spies kept a close watch on his activities, particularly looking for any evidence of seditious writings. In the summer of 1683 matters came to a head with the Rye House plot, when leading members of Shaftesbury's circle – Algernon Sydney, Lord William Russell and the Earl of Essex – were implicated in an attempt to kidnap Charles II and his brother and were all three arrested for treason, two of them subsequently being executed. Locke, though not directly involved in this conspiracy, was now even more under suspicion, and escaped to the Netherlands in September 1683. From here he did not return to England until 1689. Following the Revolutionary Settlement of 1688, which removed James II from the throne after a disastrous reign of three years, the monarchy passed jointly to the Dutch Prince of Orange, William (1650–1702), and his wife Mary (1662–94), who were James II's nephew and daughter. With the reign of the Protestant William and Mary began the long period of Whig ascendancy in English politics, a regime very much in line with Locke's own political and religious orientations.

During his last years, from his return to England in 1689 to his death in 1704, Locke enjoyed public esteem and royal favour, in addition to great intellectual fame as the author of the *Essay Concerning Human Understanding*, which was published late in 1689. He performed a number of official duties, notably as a Commissioner of the Board of Trade, though his greatest desire was to pursue his literary and intellectual interests, including a good deal of correspondence. After some years of failing health, Locke died, aged 72, at the Essex home of Sir Francis and Lady Masham, a wealthy family with whom he had resided since 1692.

Locke never married and had no children of his own, though he was fond of them and was influential in promoting more humane and rational attitudes towards their upbringing and education – never forgetting, it seems, the severe treatment he had received at Westminster

School. In character he was somewhat introverted and hypochon-driacal, but he by no means avoided company. He enjoyed good con-versation but was abstemious in his habits of eating and drinking. He was a prolific correspondent and had a great many friends and acquain-tances, on the continent of Europe as well as in Britain and Ireland. If there was a particular fault in his character, it was a slight tetchiness in reponse to criticism of his writings, even when that criticism was intended to be constructive. Though academic in his cast of mind, Locke was strongly moved by his political and religious convictions – especially by his concern for liberty and toleration – and had the good fortune to live at a time when there was no great divide between the academic pursuit of philosophical interests and the public discussion and application of political and religious principles. He thus happily lived to see some of his most strongly felt intellectual convictions realised in public policy, partly as a consequence of his own writings and involvement in public affairs.

The structure of the *Essay* and its place in Locke's work

Locke's *Essay Concerning Human Understanding*, which was first published in full in December 1689, was undoubtedly his greatest intellectual achievement. He had been working on it off and on since the early 1670s, but most intensively during his period of exile in the Netherlands between 1683 and 1689. He continued to revise it after its first appearance, supervising three further editions of it in his remain-ing years. The fourth edition of 1700 accordingly represents his final view, and is the version most closely studied today.

The *Essay* is chiefly concerned with issues in what would today be called epistemology (or the theory of knowledge), metaphysics, the philosophy of mind and the philosophy of language. As its title implies, its purpose is to discover, from an examination of the work-ings of the human mind, just what we are capable of knowing and understanding about the universe we live in. Locke's answer is that all the 'materials' of our understanding come from our 'ideas' – both of sensation and of reflection (that is, of 'outward' and 'inward' expe-rience respectively) – which are worked upon by our powers of reason to produce such 'real' knowledge as we can hope to attain. Beyond that, we have other sources of belief – for instance, in testimony and in revelation – which may afford us probability and hence warrant our assent, but do not entitle us to *certainty*.

Given these concerns, we can readily understand the overall structure of the *Essay*, which is divided into four books. Book I, 'Of Innate Notions', is devoted to an attack on the advocates of innate ideas, who held that much of our knowledge is independent of experience. In Book II, 'Of Ideas', Locke attempts to explain in some detail how sensation and reflection can in fact provide all the 'materials' of our understanding, even insofar as it embraces such relatively abstruse ideas as those of substance, identity and causality, which many of Locke's opponents took to be paradigmatically innate. In Book III, 'Of Words', Locke presents his account of how language both helps and hinders us in the communication of our ideas. Without such communication we could not hope to achieve mutual understanding, given Locke's view of the origins of our ideas in widely varying individual experience. Finally, in Book IV, 'Of Knowledge and Opinion', Locke discusses the ways in which processes of reason, learning and testimony operate upon our ideas to produce certain knowledge and probable belief, and at the same time he tries to locate the proper boundary between the province of reason and experience on the one hand and that of revelation and faith on the other.

Locke's view of our intellectual capacities is clearly a modest one. At the same time, he held a strong personal faith in the truth of Christian religious principles, which may seem to conflict with the mildly sceptical air of his epistemological doctrines. In fact, he himself perceived no conflict here – unlike some of his contemporary critics – though he did regard his modest view of our intellectual capacities as providing a strong motive for religious toleration. Reason, he thought, does not conflict with faith, but in questions of faith to which reason supplies no answer it is both irrational and immoral to insist on conformity of belief. We have it on record, indeed, that what orginally motivated Locke to pursue the inquiries of the *Essay* was precisely a concern to settle how far reason and experience could take us in determining moral and religious truths.

Locke's concern with morality and religion, both intimately bound up with questions of political philosophy in the seventeenth century, was one which dominated his thinking throughout his intellectual and public career. His earliest works, unpublished in his own lifetime, were the *Two Tracts on Government* (1660 and 1661) and the *Essays on the Law of Nature* (1664), both written in Latin but now available in English translation. The position on issues of political liberty and religious toleration which he adopted in those early works was, however, considerably more conservative than the one that he later came to espouse, following his association with Shaftesbury, and made famous in his *Letter on Toleration* and *Two Treatises of Government* (both published, anonymously, in 1689, the former in Latin and the latter in English). The *Second Treatise* explicitly recognises the right of subjects to overthrow even a legitimately appointed ruler who has abused his trust and tyrannises his people – a doctrine which would almost certainly have led to Locke's being accused of sedition had the manuscript been discovered by government spies. The *First Treatise* was an extended attack upon an ultra-royalist tract written by Sir Robert Filmer (d. 1653), entitled *Patriarcha* (published 1680), in which the divine right of kings was defended as proceeding from the dominion first granted by God to Adam. Algernon Sydney (1622–83), one of the Rye House plot conspirators, had been convicted of sedition partly on the strength of a manuscript he had written attacking Filmer's work, so one can well understand Locke's secrecy and caution in the years preceding his flight to the Netherlands.

In addition to the works already mentioned, Locke published a good many other writings, notably on religious and educational topics. *Some Thoughts Concerning Education* (1693) was the product of advice he had provided in correspondence, over a number of years, to his friends Edward and Mary Clarke concerning the upbringing of their children. This work went into many editions, proving to be very popular and influential with more enlightened parents for a long time to come. Locke's interest in the intellectual development of children is also plain to see in the *Essay* itself, where it has a direct relevance to his empiricist principles of learning and of concept-formation.

Locke's explicitly religious writings include *The Reasonableness of Christianity* (1695) and the learned and very substantial *Paraphrase and Notes on the Epistles of St Paul* (published posthumously, 1705–7). He also wrote on economic and monetary issues connected with his various involvements in public and political affairs. He even found time to compose a critique of the theories of the French philosopher Nicholas Malebranche (1638–1715, a contemporary developer of Cartesian philosophy), entitled *An Examination of P. Malebranche's Opinion of Seeing All Things in God.* Other items included in his collected *Works*, which have run to many editions, are lengthy replies to Edward Stillingfleet (1635–99), bishop of Worcester, answering hostile criticisms raised by the latter against the *Essay*, and a long piece entitled 'Of the Conduct of the Understanding', which was originally intended for inclusion in a later edition of the *Essay*.

From this brief survey of Locke's work, we see that although his most important writings were published in his fifties and sixties, during a comparatively short interval beginning in his most famous year of 1689, his thoughts were the product of a very long period of gestation stretching back at least thirty years before that. It is quite fair to say, however, that the *Essay* was the cornerstone of all his intellectual activity, providing the epistemological and methodological framework for all his other views and enterprises. And although we are particularly fortunate in having a remarkably complete collection of Locke's original manuscripts and letters as well as his many other publications, it is on the *Essay* that his reputation as the greatest English philosopher stands. Written in English at a time when English prose style was at the peak of its vigour, and Latin had begun to wane as the language of intellectual communication, it is both a literary and a philosophical masterpiece, which can still be read today for pleasure as well as enlightenment. Although in reading the *Essay* it is a help to know something of the historical and intellectual background to its composition, it is a remarkable testimony to its durability and stature as a work of philosophy, as well as to its appeal as a work of literature, that it can still be taken up and studied with profit and pleasure, three hundred years after its first appearance, by anyone susceptible to the intellectual curiosity which its content provokes.

Contemporary reception of the *Essay*

Locke's *Essay* aroused widespread attention from the moment it first appeared. One reason for this was the excellent publicity it received in the leading intellectual journals of the day (at a time when academic journals were a comparatively recent phenomenon). An abridged version, prepared by Locke himself, actually appeared in 1688 – a year before the full text was published – in an internationally renowned journal, the *Bibliothèque universelle.* Many contemporary philosophers, including Leibniz, became acquainted with Locke's work by this means. The first edition of the full text was published in London late in 1689, and soon received appreciative reviews in various widely read journals. Between 1689 and 1700, Locke was to prepare three further, extensively revised editions of the *Essay*. A French translation by Pierre Coste appeared in 1700, soon followed by a Latin translation; both of these were vitally important in disseminating Locke's ideas amongst European intellectuals. From all this publishing activity, it is clear that from the very beginning the *Essay* was recognised very widely as being a major work of philosophy.

In these early years, reaction to the *Essay* was deeply divided, some critics eulogising it while others were deeply hostile. For a time hostility mounted, but it later subsided as broadly Lockean views in epistemology and metaphysics began to become widely accepted. The intial hostility was directed at features of the *Essay* thought by some to be damaging to religion (and, by implication, to morality) – notably, its apparently sceptical air and its repudiation of *innate ideas*. Although Locke himself had a strong Protestant faith, he was suspected by some of favouring a version of Christian doctrine known as Socinianism, which involved a denial of the Trinity. Such a view might be regarded as a natural precursor of the *deism* that was to become widespread amongst enlightened intellectuals in the eighteenth century. Deism was to be a rationalistic but somewhat sanitised and watered-down conception of monotheism which attempted to eliminate all the more mysterious and miraculous features of traditional religious belief, and was itself just a staging-post on the way towards the wholly secular, atheistic world-view taken for granted in most Western intellectual circles today.

Of course, Locke cannot be held responsible for this gradual slide to atheism, and there is no doubt at all about the sincerity of his own Christian faith, but his early critics may well have been right in seeing dangers to their conception of religion in the emphasis Locke laid upon reason and experience in the foundations of human knowledge. Of this sort of critic, Edward Stillingfleet, the bishop of Worcester, was perhaps the most formidable, and he and Locke engaged in a series of substantial published exchanges.

It is perhaps hard for us today to see Locke as a particularly sceptical philosopher, especially when we compare him with David Hume (1711–76), whose *Treatise of Human Nature* of 1739 was quite self-consciously sceptical in its approach, and indeed sceptical about most of the claims central to Locke's realism concerning the world of material objects. Locke was really not so much sceptical as anti-dogmatic, notably about religious claims based on revelation rather than on reason and experience. But to the religious dogmatists of his time, this would indeed have appeared dangerously sceptical. Locke's attack on the doctrine of innate ideas undoubtedly added to these suspicions. Adherents of that doctrine held that the concept of God, and related moral and religious principles, were actually planted in our minds from birth by God Himself, giving us no excuse for denying their veracity. To repudiate the doctrine therefore struck many as opening the floodgates to atheism and immorality. Of course, nothing could have been further from Locke's intention: his motive for attacking the doctrine of innate ideas – apart from the fact that he thought it was simply false – was that he saw it as a socially and intellectually pernicious buttress for all sorts of obscurantist and authoritarian views. In Locke's opinion, God gave mankind sense organs and a power of reason in order to discover such knowledge (including *moral* knowledge) as we need to have, thus rendering innate ideas quite unnecessary. And in matters of faith which go beyond the reach of reason and experience, revelation is only a ground for private, individual religious belief, which it would be morally as well as intellectually wrong to make enforceable universally by the authority of church or state.

Amongst the contemporary philosophical – as opposed to religious – critics of the *Essay*, two deserve special mention: the Irishman George Berkeley (1685–1753), bishop of Cloyne, and the German polymath Gottfried Wilhelm Leibniz (1646–1716). Much of Berkeley's philosophy, notably his *Principles of Human Knowledge* of 1713, can be seen as a reaction to Locke's. Berkeley was like some other Christian critics of the *Essay* in attacking what he saw as its potential for scepticism, but unlike them focused on what Locke himself would have regarded as the *least* sceptical aspect of his position – his realism concerning the world of material objects. Berkeley saw the real threat to religion in Locke's position as lying in its advocacy of a material world existing independently of any mind (including, at least potentially, the mind of God). He also thought that to regard the 'real' world as being somehow divested of all the sensible qualities of colour, sound, taste and smell which characterise our immediate experience of things, apparently making it a lifeless realm of atoms moving in the void, was just to invite doubts about the very existence of anything beyond our own private experience. As we shall see, Berkeley's criticisms of Locke, though sometimes based on what appear to be mistaken or uncharitable interpretations of Locke's views, do raise serious questions which are hard to answer – even if Berkeley's own 'idealist' alternative may strike us as still harder to defend.

Leibniz, unlike Berkeley, criticised Locke's views during Locke's own lifetime, both in printed pieces and in correspondence. Locke was acquainted with some of these criticisms, but appears not to have been much taken with them, despite Leibniz's very considerable reputation in European intellectual circles at the time. Leibniz even wrote an extended work in dialogue form, discussing the *Essay* chapter by chapter, entitled *New Essays on Human Understanding* – but he gave up plans to publish it upon learning of Locke's death in 1704. In due course this important work was, however, published, and it contains many insightful criticisms of Locke's views, as well as clarifying Leibniz's own opinions on many matters. Some of Leibniz's most memorable criticisms are directed against Locke's attack on innate ideas. Leibniz – like René Descartes (1591–1650) before him – defended the doctrine of innate ideas not in any spirit of authoritarian dogmatism or obscurantism, but rather because he considered that certain fundamental components of human knowledge and understanding could not simply be acquired, as Locke believed, from sense-experience. In answer to Locke's challenge to explain in what sense knowledge could be said to be 'in' the mind of an infant who was apparently quite unaware of it, Leibniz was to adopt a strikingly modern conception of cognition as being in quite large measure a subconscious process – a view which, in our own post-Freudian age, may appear less contentious than it would have done to Locke's contemporaries, many of whom (Locke included) were strongly influenced by Descartes's conception of the mind as being in every way consciously knowable to itself.

In sum, we see that Locke's *Essay* received close attention by the very best minds of his time, and rapidly achieved an eminence which it has never since lost amongst the classics of Western philosophy. Despite initially being banned at Oxford University as dangerous material for students to read, it soon became a standard text and lost its early notoriety as a radical and even revolutionary work. It often happens with revolutionary writings that once their tenets have been absorbed into the prevailing orthodoxy, they begin to appear quite conservative, and become targets themselves for later revolutionaries – as the *Essay* did for eighteenth-century philosophers like Hume.

The place of the *Essay* in the history of philosophy

It is significant that while Descartes and Locke both use architectural metaphors to characterise their respective philosophical enterprises, Descartes (for instance, in the *Meditations* of 1641) casts himself in the role of both designer and builder of the new edifice of scientific knowledge, whereas Locke assumes the humbler position of an 'under-labourer' clearing the ground of rubbish in order that others – like Newton, Boyle and Huygens – can build anew more effectively. (See Locke's Epistle to the Reader, which prefaces the *Essay*.) This difference reflects significantly different conceptions of the proper relationship between philosophy and the sciences. Descartes saw metaphysics as providing an a priori foundation for the special sciences, and epistemology as prescribing the correct scientific method. By contrast, Locke conceded far more autonomy and authority to the practitioners of science themselves and saw the philosopher's task, insofar as it impinges upon science, more as one of exposing the inflated and nonsensical claims of those who pretend to knowledge without conducting adequate scientific research. Locke's view of the proper relationship between science and philosophy has now become a tacit assumption of mainstream modern thought, helping to define the very distinction between 'philosophical' and 'scientific' inquiry. But we should not forget that in Locke's own day the terms 'science' and 'philosophy' were not presumed to denote quite distinct disciplines, and indeed were often used interchangeably. For better or worse, we partly owe this shift in usage to the influence of philosophers like Locke.

It is common for Locke and Descartes to be classified, respectively, as 'empiricist' and 'rationalist' philosophers, other 'rationalists' being Spinoza (1632–77) and Leibniz, while other 'empiricists' are Berkeley and Hume. However, this terminology has now begun to fall into disrepute, for the very good reason that it serves to mask quite as many similarities and differences as it serves to highlight. On all sorts of specific issues, it is possible to find an 'empiricist' philosopher like Locke agreeing more with a 'rationalist' philosopher like Descartes than he does with another philosopher who is supposedly a fellow 'empiricist'. Furthermore, even when the empiricist/rationalist distinction is only used to focus on differences within its proper sphere of epistemology, it can have a distorting influence – as when Descartes is erroneously presumed to espouse a wholly aprioristic view of scientific inquiry, as capable of being conducted without any reference to experiment or observation, or when it is forgotten that most of what Locke regards as 'real' knowledge (for instance, mathematical and moral knowledge) is viewed by him as being a product of intuition and reason rather than of learning from experience. If there *is* a single epistemological doctrine uniting all the so-called empiricists against all the so-called rationalists, it is the former's denial of the existence of *innate* ideas and knowledge. But, ironically enough – as we shall see in Chapter 2 – it turns out that not nearly so much of importance hinges upon this denial as Locke and his fellow 'empiricists' thought. To the extent that 'empiricism' denotes a distinctive philosophical position worth defending, it is in fact perfectly possible to be an empiricist while accepting the existence of innate ideas – indeed, while accepting their existence on *empirical* grounds.

Altogether, then, it is *not* helpful to try to locate the position of Locke's *Essay* within the history of philosophy by simplistically describing it as 'the first great empiricist text' (a description which would, in any case, serve to undervalue or ignore the earlier contributions of Bacon, Hobbes and Gassendi). And yet it seems clear that the

Essay not only *was* (and is) a work of major philosophical importance, but also that it does mark a watershed in philosophical thought and the beginning of a new philosophical tradition. (It is clear also, despite my earlier warnings, that the 'empiricist' label is not wholly inappropriate.) What is distinctive of this new tradition both reflected in and inspired by the *Essay* is precisely the shift, mentioned earlier, that it recognises in the relationship between philosophy and the sciences. By the end of the seventeenth century, the natural sciences had begun to assert their own autonomy and to develop their own distinctive procedures and institutions, and philosophy in the shape of metaphysics and epistemology could no longer (as in Descartes's day) presume to dictate how inquiry into the nature and workings of the physical world should proceed, much less to supply answers to specific questions in that field. It is to Locke's great credit that he was amongst the first to perceive this, and consequently amongst the first to reconceptualise the role of philosophy as having chiefly a *critical* function, adjudicating knowledge-claims rather than providing their primary source.

We see this conception of the proper role of philosophical inquiry even more self-consciously adopted by Locke's successors, notably by Hume, but above all by Immanuel Kant (1724–1804) – who, somewhat unfairly, largely claimed for himself the credit for having invented 'critical' philosophy. Kant tends to divide his predecessors into 'dogmatists' and 'sceptics', but even if Hume often seems to merit the latter label, it is surely clear that Locke merits neither. That is what gives Locke's philosophy such a modern cast and such a lasting value. He does not claim that philosophy can provide definitive answers to substantive questions about the nature of reality, but at the same time he denies any pretension on the part of philosophy to undermine altogether our claims to natural knowledge. Philosophy cannot provide all the answers to our queries, but nor can it assure us that none is to be had. Its task, rather, is to remind us that in pursuing knowledge of the world we must take into account the nature and limitations of those very faculties of ours – for perception and reason – which enable us to acquire knowledge at all, and to recall that we too are part of the world whose nature we desire to understand.

This self-reflective, critical turn in the orientation of philosophical inquiry, though partly prefigured in some of Descartes's writings, arguably finds its first clear expression in Locke's *Essay Concerning Human Understanding* – whose very title, indeed, proclaims this change of perspective. Even if Locke was quite as much a mouthpiece for an independently occurring shift in intellectual opinion as a maker of such a shift, the *Essay* must be hailed as a landmark of immense significance in the history of ideas, as marking a turning-point whose repercussions are still being worked out in philosophical debate today. It is unsurprising, then, that on so many hotly disputed current issues – such as the concept of personal identity, the problem of 'free will' and the relation between language and thought – philosophers still turn to the *Essay* as a starting-point for their arguments.

Chapter 2

Ideas

The historical background to Locke's critique of innatism

Who believed in the doctrine of innate ideas, and why? And why was Locke so keen to attack it? Certainly, the doctrine already had in Locke's time a long philosophical pedigree, traceable back at least as far as Plato. In Plato's philosophy, the doctrine is associated with a transcendent metaphysics: the theory of Forms and a belief in the immateriality and pre-existence of the soul. Plato considered that the objects of true knowledge – of which mathematical knowledge was for him the paradigm – could not belong to the imperfect and confused world of sensory experience, and that the human mind or soul must therefore possess a means of access to such knowledge independent of experience. In a famous passage in one of his dialogues, the *Meno*, he portrays Socrates eliciting the proof of a geometrical theorem from an untutored slave boy, merely by the judicious posing of questions. This was supposed to

show that the boy already implicitly knew the proof, and that (as Plato argues in the *Phaedo*) the ultimate source of such knowledge must be the acquaintance of the soul with the mathematical Forms in a previous existence. The Platonic Forms – also somewhat misleadingly called 'Ideas' – were supposedly ideal types existing in a separate, non-physical realm, examples being the perfect shapes of geometry – circles, triangles and squares – which are only imperfectly approximated to by physical objects.

Platonism had been overshadowed by the influence of Aristotle during the mediaeval period, despite the obvious affinity of transcendent metaphysics with certain aspects of Christian doctrine (such as the belief in a spiritual afterlife). And Aristotle was very much a down-to-earth empiricist and, in today's terms, a physicalist. Many of his mediaeval scholastic followers espoused empiricism, as encapsulated in the Latin phrase *nihil est in intellectu quod non fuerit in sensu* ('nothing is in the understanding which was not previously encountered in sense-experience'). They often combined this doctrine with either nominalism or conceptualism – both involving a denial of the transcendent reality of independent Forms or universals (see pp. 162–3) – and with a repudiation of Plato's conception of the soul as a separate entity pre-existing the body.

However, during the Renaissance there had been some revival of Platonist views – or, more exactly, of Neoplatonist views, filtered through the late classical writings of Plotinus and Porphyry (see Copenhaver & Schmitt 1992, ch. 3). In some ways, such views were more in keeping with the spirit of the age than were those of the mediaeval schoolmen. For one thing, Plato placed great emphasis on the importance of mathematics – especially geometry – in our understanding of the nature of the world, and during the Renaissance period mathematical knowledge and its applications were beginning to develop apace. The fruits of this growth could be found in the astronomical and mechanical theories of Kepler, Copernicus and Galileo, and thus ultimately in the 'new science' of the seventeenth century. This new science was totally at odds with the non-mathematical approach to nature characteristic of Aristotelianism and promised to be much more useful in explaining and predicting physical phenomena, a better understanding of which was crucial for technological advances in artillery, chronometry and navigation.

Thus, surprisingly enough, the seemingly unworldly transcendent metaphysics and epistemology of Plato promised to have more practical application than those of the empirically minded Aristotle. But, at the same time, this shift of emphasis produced something of a crisis in the theory of knowledge. If the long-standing authority of Aristotle and the Bible had begun to be found wanting, and progress lay instead in the mathematical understanding of nature, what, ultimately, could provide the underpinning and guarantee of the reliability of this new route to knowledge? Sense experience, favoured by Aristotle, had proved to be an unreliable guide. This is vividly exemplified by mediaeval illustrations of the supposed trajectories of cannon-balls, which deviate greatly from the parabolic paths which Galileo correctly argued that they must follow. (It is, incidentally, a myth that Galileo 'proved' that objects with different weights fall at the same rate by dropping them from the leaning tower of Pisa – that is, by observation. Rather, he demonstrated this by an a priori thought experiment (see Galileo 1954, pp. 62ff.)!)

It was in this context of epistemological crisis that Descartes sought a new foundation for the new science, a foundation independent of untrustworthy sense-experience and the failed authority of Aristotle. Though not explicitly a Platonist himself, Descartes's philosophy has many affinities with that of Plato – belief in the pre-eminence of mathematical knowledge, in the existence of a separate, immaterial soul, and in the presence within that soul of 'innate ideas' being three key resemblances. But where Plato had appealed to the soul's pre-existing acquaintance with the Forms as the source of its innate knowledge, Descartes instead, with his Christian heritage, appealed to the benevolence of the soul's creator, God. God it was who 'imprinted' in the soul ideas of substance, causation, geometry and, above all, Himself, by recourse to which human beings are able to discover the path to true and certain knowledge of other features of God's created world.

Now Locke was no enemy of the new science himself, and no friend of Aristotelian scholastic philosophy. Why, then, was he so hostile to the doctrine of innate ideas? One reason, perhaps, is that in Britain, as opposed to the continent of Europe, the new science of the seventeenth century had already been given a more empiricist cast by the writings of Francis Bacon (1561–1626) on the one hand, and by the scientific work of such experimentalists as Hooke, Boyle and Newton on the other. Bacon, in his *Novum organum* (1620), had recommended that we discover Nature's secrets by interrogating her systematically – essentially, by applying an inductive method of discovery through controlled experiment and observation. And the early members of the Royal Society had, by the time of Locke's *Essay*, already made considerable headway in unlocking Nature's secrets by just such careful investigation. Newton, of course, was himself a mathematician, who fully believed in the mathematisation of natural phenomena – but, unlike the aprioristic Descartes, he recognised the need for mathematical theories to be answerable to empirical observation. Locke saw his role as a philosopher as that of a 'humble under-labourer' clearing the way for scientists like Newton to uncover the workings of the natural world through the application of mathematical theory to careful empirical inquiry – he did not have the ambition of Descartes to provide an a priori foundation for science in metaphysics and epistemology.

Another, and perhaps even more important, reason for Locke's hostility to the doctrine of innate ideas was, however, the danger which lay in it to freedom of thought and inquiry, not only in science but also in matters of morality, religion and politics. By contrast to the quietist Descartes, Locke was a champion of individual liberty and rights at a time when these were, in Britain at least, enjoying a precarious flowering. Absolute monarchy, in the shape of the Stuarts, had received a rebuff during the Civil War, only to be revived in a milder form with the Restoration. Locke was on the winning side when the Stuarts were finally removed in 1688–9 with the so-called Glorious Revolution. But political and religious liberty was still very much a delicate flower. Now, the docrine of innate ideas is inherently prone to exploitation by conservative and reactionary forces, because it is only too easy to appeal to supposedly God-given principles of morality and religion to attempt to silence challenges to prevailing authority and interests. This potential of the doctrine for abuse by illiberal forces clearly weighed heavily with Locke in determining him to oppose it. Indeed, it may have weighed too heavily, in the sense that it may have prejudiced him against some of the legitimate grounds for defence of certain forms of the doctrine. There is an irony in the fact that Locke himself, so keen to defend the pursuit of truth by free inquiry, may have done injustice to the doctrine of innate ideas on account of the danger he perceived it to harbour.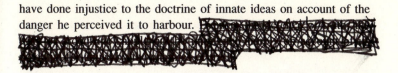

Locke's uses of the term 'idea'

I have spoken of Locke as attacking the doctrine of innate *ideas*, and indeed he does at times write in these terms – though he also writes about the supposition of innate 'notions' and 'principles'. But before we can proceed we need to be clearer about this slippery term 'idea', which was so prolifically used in seventeenth-century works on metaphysics and epistemology, with a range of fairly precise technical meanings, most of them now superseded or regarded as questionable.

One way in which Locke does *not* use the term 'idea' is in the Platonic sense, to denote a transcendent Form (and when it is understood in this sense, confusion is best avoided by writing 'Idea' with a capital *I*). For Locke, ideas are subjective, mental phenomena – although he acknowledges (2.8.8) that he sometimes carelessly uses the term 'idea' to denote a *quality* of a physical object existing external to the mind. (We should not lose sight of this usage, even though Locke himself repudiates it, because later empiricists – notably, the 'idealist' Berkeley – were to argue for an *identity* between ideas and qualities, denying that the latter are, as Locke thought, properties of mind-independent objects.)

Locke defines an idea as 'Whatsoever the Mind perceives in itself, or is the immediate object of Perception, Thought or Understanding' (2.8.8), and in doing so he may appear to be guilty of running together two quite distinct fields of mental phenomena – namely, *percepts* and *concepts*. When we enjoy sensory experiences of our physical environment – for instance, by opening our eyes and looking at surrounding objects – we are conscious of being subject to states of qualitative awareness. For example, when a normally sighted person sees a red and a green object in ordinary daylight, he or she will enjoy distinctive qualities of colour experience – 'qualia', in the modern jargon – which will be absent from the perceptual experience of a red–green colour-blind person in the same circumstances. Locke seems at least sometimes to be using the term 'idea' to refer to such experiential qualia. However, he also uses the term at times to refer to what we would now call *concepts* – that is, the meaningful components of the thoughts we entertain privately and attempt to communicate to one another in language. The latter sense of 'idea' is indeed still a commonplace of everyday usage, as when we say that someone has no *idea* of what the word 'trigonometry' means.

Now, it would be precipitate to accuse Locke at this stage of a *confusion* between percepts and concepts, first of all because the latter distinction is itself one of philosophical making and thus not immune to criticism, but also because it is part of Locke's very project in the *Essay* to forge a link between perceptual experience and our intellectual resources – a link which would, if it can be sustained, blur this very distinction. Thus, although a later empiricist, Hume, does indeed draw a distinction between what he calls 'ideas' and 'impressions', which appears roughly to coincide with a concept/percept divide, even he does not regard this as serving to distinguish between two radically different *kinds* of mental phenomena – indeed, he talks of ideas as being 'copies' of impressions, and differing from them only in their degree of 'vivacity'. Locke's main aim in the *Essay* is precisely to demonstrate the truth of empiricism, by showing how the 'materials' of thought and understanding all have their origin in perceptual experience (which, we should remember, he takes to embrace not only sensation but also 'reflection' on 'the internal Operations of our Minds' (2.1.2)). On this kind of account, concepts are indeed intimately related to percepts.

For many modern philosophers, however, this Lockean approach is utterly untenable, for various reasons. One is that they are often – though rather less so of late – dubious about the epistemological status or even the very existence of sensory qualia, and therefore regard ideas in this sense as an unpromising starting-point for the philosophy of mind and the theory of knowledge. Another reason is that they consider it a naive mistake to regard 'concepts' as introspectible mental phenomena which are the materials or ingredients of thought. Rather, concepts are, they hold, more like *abilities*, especially linguistic abilities to deploy certain words appropriately in successful communication. Knowing the meaning of a word, on this model, is not being acquainted with some Lockean idea, but is, rather, knowing how to *use* the word correctly according to public, intersubjective standards. My own opinion is that there is more to be said for Locke's view than these modern critics allow, for reasons which will emerge in later sections.

One particular issue that we shall need to confront is the question of what precisely Locke means by describing ideas as 'immediate objects' of mental processes – both what he understands by 'immediacy' and what he intends by 'object'. In calling ideas *objects*, should he be construed as regarding them as *images* – as it were, mental pictures available for scrutiny by the mind's 'inner eye'? At any rate, is he at least treating ideas as *things* of some sort, to which the perceiving or thinking mind stands in some genuine relationship (of 'grasping', or perceiving, or whatnot)? Again, in speaking of them as *immediate* objects, is he implying that our awareness of *other*, 'external' objects is *mediated by* our awareness of ideas, which thus constitute some sort of screen or veil between us and those other objects? And if so, does this harbour sceptical problems which serve to promote the cause of idealism? My answer will be that Locke should probably *not* be construed as treating ideas as 'thinglike', but that in any case this issue has no real bearing on the problem of scepticism, which arises equally for the so-called 'direct realist'.

Before we proceed to examine Locke's arguments against the doctrine of innate ideas, mention should be made of the doctrine he intends to put in its place – a doctrine which we can go on calling, for want of a better word, 'empiricism'. (In point of fact, there are many different varieties of empiricism, but this need not concern us at present.) Locke's empiricism is at once *atomistic* and *constructivist*. In calling it 'atomistic', I mean that Locke regards ideas as falling into two classes, *simple* and *complex*, with complex ideas being analysable into simple components. For instance, the idea of a perceptible quality like redness is, for Locke, simple: our concept of redness cannot be analysed into any simpler elements – unlike, for example, our concept of a horse, which can. In calling Locke's doctrine 'constructivist', I mean this: he holds that all of our ideas (= concepts) ultimately 'derive' from experience, that is, from *percepts* – but he does not hold that in order to possess a given complex idea (= concept), one must have enjoyed a correspondingly complex percept, since it suffices for one to have enjoyed the various simple percepts corresponding to the simple ideas (= concepts) into which that complex idea is analysable. Thus one can possess the concept of a *unicorn* despite never having perceived such a creature (or even a mock-up of one), because it is analysable in terms of simpler concepts (those of a horse and a horn) which themselves either answer to experience or are further analysable in terms of concepts which *are* thus answerable.

Notice that while atomism and constructivism go well together, neither entails the other. One could be a constructivist and yet deny that there are any conceptual 'simples'. Alternatively, one could believe in conceptual simples and yet insist that complex concepts cannot be acquired in the absence of correspondingly complex perceptual experience. In the course of the *Essay*, Locke attempts to make good his claim to provide an alternative to innatism by analysing some of the key concepts – like that of *substance* – which innatists held to be innate, and endeavouring to show how their simple ingredients might be acquired from experience and then put together by the intellect.

Locke's arguments against innate ideas

Some preliminary distinctions need to be made concerning the objects of Locke's attack. Although loosely an attack on innate ideas, Locke's onslaught is mainly aimed against supposedly innate *principles* and only secondarily against innate *notions*, which seem to be equivalent to ideas (= concepts). A principle is something *propositional* in form, as Locke makes clear by two of his favourite examples, 'those magnified Principles of Demonstration, *Whatsoever is, is*; and *'Tis impossible for the same thing to be, and not to be'* (1.2.4). By contrast, an idea, or notion, or concept is only an ingredient or component of a proposition (or of the meaning of a sentence expressing a proposition). Evidently, now, if a 'principle' is innate, every idea or concept contained in it must likewise be innate, so that innate principles imply innate ideas, as Locke himself remarks (1.4.1). But the reverse may not be so: it would apparently be possible to maintain that certain ideas or concepts are innate while denying that any of the principles in which they figure are innate. Locke, however, does not give serious consid-eration to this possibility, focusing his attack chiefly upon principles and even, at one point, presuming the absurdity of supposing there to be innate ideas as a supplementary reason for rejecting the supposition of innate principles (1.4.3).

Another distinction deserving some comment is the distinction Locke draws between *speculative* and *practical* principles. The former are logical and metaphysical principles – like the two already cited – whereas the latter concern morality, that is, our duties to one another and to God. Our attention in what follows will be concentrated on the former, though it is clear that in terms of the danger to freedom posed by innatist doctrines, innatism regarding the principles of morality, politics and religion must have been of more urgent concern to Locke.

It has to be said that, for all his confident rhetoric and heavy sarcasm, Locke's explicit arguments against innatism are not markedly cogent. These arguments focus on the issue of 'universal consent' (or 'assent'). Locke seems to presume (a) that the proponents of innate principles believe that these principles are universally assented to by all mankind; (b) that this universal assent is supposed to be clear proof of the innate status of these principles; and (c) that there is no other evidence that is or can be offered in support of the innateness of any principle. In characterising his opponents' position in this highly uncharitable way, Locke is already guilty of setting up something of a straw man for his target.

For example, as regards b above, Locke remarks at one point:

> [Even] if it were true in matter of Fact, that there were certain Truths, wherein all Mankind agreed, it would not prove them innate, if there can be any other way shewn, how Men may come to that Universal Agreement. (1.2.3)

Of course, Locke is right that a hypothesis is never *conclusively proved* to be correct by any evidence which *could* be explained by another, rival hypothesis: but it may still be the case that such evidence *sup-ports the first hypothesis more strongly* than any of its rivals, because that hypothesis explains the evidence more economically than they do. This is a style of non-demonstrative reasoning, known as 'inference to the best explanation' (or 'abduction'), which is common in many scientific contexts in which complete certainty or 'proof' is not attainable. Thus it is still open to the innatist, Locke's criticism notwithstanding, to urge that universal assent to certain principles is better explained by, and thus more strongly supports, the doctrine of innatism than any rival hypothesis. But Locke unfairly tends to assume that innatism must be an explanation of the last resort, inherently inferior to any conceivable alternative explanation.

As regards point c above – Locke's assumption that the innatist has nothing else to appeal to but universal assent – this makes itself manifest in a curious inversion which Locke attempts to impose on the innatist's supposed argument from universal assent. Confident that there are in fact *no* principles which receive universal assent, Locke claims that this demonstrates that there are after all no innate principles:

> this Argument of Universal Consent, which is made use of, to prove innate Principles, seems to me a Demonstration that there are none such: Because there are none to which all Mankind give an Universal Assent. (1.2.4)

On the face of it, this is a blatant example of the fallacy of 'denying the antecedent'. The innatist, Locke has suggested, makes the following claim:

1. If any principle is universally assented to, then it is innate.

The innatist then allegedly conjoins 1 with the claim that certain principles *are* universally assented to, and validly draws the conclusion that those principles are innate. But Locke himself now *denies* the antecedent of 1 by asserting:

2. No principle is universally assented to;

and concludes thence

3. No principle is innate.

But 1 and 2 do *not* entail 3. (To suppose that they do is precisely to commit the fallacy of 'denying the antecedent'.) What is needed in conjunction with 2 to entail 3 is, rather,

4. If any principle is innate, then it is universally assented to.

But why should the innatist be committed to the truth of 4? It is of no use in his supposed 'argument from universal assent' – an argument which, as we have just seen, uses 1 instead. Of course, 1 and 4 are by no means equivalent. (Locke himself, I should mention, *does* explicitly endorse 4, saying, for instance, that 'universal Assent . . . must needs be the necessary concomitant of all innate Truths' (1.2.5) – but this is not demanded by the logic of the innatist's argument, which is what is here at issue.)

However, a justification of Locke's strategy may be forthcoming if we take him to suppose that the innatist has and can have *nothing other* than universal assent to offer in support of the existence of innate principles. For if that were the innatist's position, he would indeed do well *not* to deny 4, that is, not to allow that there might be innate principles that are not universally assented to. For in the case of these principles, evidence for their existence in the form of universal assent would be, *ex hypothesi*, not available: but then, in conjunction with the supposition that *nothing but* universal assent is evidence for innateness, this would condemn the innatist to conceding that there was *no evidence at all* in favour of the allegedly innate principles in question.

But we have still to address the central question of whether or not any principles *are* in fact universally assented to. Against this claim, Locke makes the preliminary remark (1.2.5) that ''tis evident, that all *Children*, and *Ideots*, have not the least Apprehension or Thought of' the principles claimed to be innate – principles such as 'Whatsoever is, is' and ''Tis impossible for the same thing to be, and not to be' (which we may construe to be, respectively, the law of identity and the law of non-contradiction). This remark, however, is not very compelling, because 'assent' need not always be explicit (indeed, in his *Second Treatise of Government* Locke himself makes extensive use of the notion of *tacit* consent). All that is 'evident' is that children and 'idiots' do not *expressly affirm* the principles in question: but that is not enough to show that they do not somehow 'apprehend', and in that sense, 'assent to' those principles. All that Locke has to offer here is the blustering comment that it seems to him 'near a Contradiction, to say, that there are Truths imprinted on the Soul, which it perceives or understands not' (1.2.5). But what he *needs* to argue at this stage is, rather, that the soul – for instance, of a child or an idiot – cannot perceive or understand a truth which it is incapable of expressly assenting to.

Of course, it is incumbent upon the innatist to say what sort of evidence *would* point to a child's 'tacit' assent to, say, the law of non-contradiction. One suggestion which Locke considers is that evidence of this is provided by the alleged fact that young people *do* eventually give express assent to such a law, when asked, *upon attaining the use of reason*. But he makes light work of dismissing this as vacuous, on the grounds that no distinction could then be made between supposedly innate principles and a host of other obvious truths – such as that white is not black – to which immediate assent will also be expressly given by a child who has reached that age. (The presumption here seems to be that very young infants do *not* in fact engage in reasoning – though this seems highly questionable. Again, we should not confuse the possession of an intellectual skill with an ability to deploy it verbally.)

Perhaps the most interesting challenge that Locke presents to the innatist comes when he claims that 'No proposition can be said to be in the Mind, which it never yet knew, which it was never yet conscious of' (1.2.5). Clearly, Locke is here allowing that we do not need to be *presently* conscious of every proposition 'in' our mind. Some truths of which we are not presently conscious we can 'call to mind', because they are stored 'in' our memory – but, according to Locke, we must have been conscious of them at *some* past time in order for them to have been 'stored' in the first place. It is interesting to recall here that Plato himself actually used the model of memory to describe the soul's relationship to its innate knowledge – the soul 'remembers' the Forms with which it was acquainted prior to its union with the body. So Plato would presumably *agree* with Locke's point in the quoted remark, and just insist against him that the child (or its soul) *was* once conscious of, say, the truth of the law of non-contradiction. Barring disproof of the doctrine of metempsychosis (the transmigration of souls), Locke has no conclusive argument against this possibility.

In the next section, I shall try to indicate how a modern innatist might attempt to rise to Locke's challenge. An important point which can, however, be drawn from Locke is that it will not be enough for the innatist simply to say that a proposition can be innately 'in' the mind in virtue of the mind's having a *capacity* to understand it – for, as Locke remarks, by that standard, 'all Propositions that are true, and the Mind is capable ever of assenting to, may be said to be in the Mind' (1.2.5), rendering the innatist's thesis trivial. This may be seen as Locke's reply to those of his contemporaries, like Descartes, who thought of innate knowledge as somehow being a *latent* or *dormant* state requiring only the mind's maturation and exposure to appropriate experience for its release or activation. Thus Descartes suggests, in *Comments on a Certain Broadsheet*, the model of a congenital disease, present from birth, whose symptoms only emerge later in life; and even Leibniz, in the *New Essays* (1981, p. 52), offers the famous analogy of a block of marble in which a yet-to-be-formed statue is prefigured by faults and veins in the stone. The trouble with both of these models of innate knowledge is that they fail adequately to distinguish between the presence of an innate *capacity* for knowledge (which Locke by no means wishes to deny) and the presence of *actual* knowledge in the mind of an infant from birth. Only the latter properly deserves to be called innate knowledge. (It is true that, as I mentioned in the section at pp. 7–11 above, Leibniz thought that many of our cognitive processes are subconscious, and this gives him the resources for a conception of innate knowledge which is much less vulnerable to Locke's line of criticism than is Descartes's; but, even so, the analogy of the block of marble clearly suffers from the difficulty just mentioned.)

A modern nativist's response to Locke

Although Locke's arguments against innate ideas and principles are far from compelling, nonetheless it is incumbent upon his opponents to explain in what sense such ideas and principles may be said to be 'in' the mind of a person even at a time when that person is incapable of giving explicit expression to them. It is likewise necessary for these opponents to tell us what sort of evidence supports their view, and how. In the remainder of this chapter I shall call these envisaged opponents of Locke *nativists*, but I shall be more concerned with the modern case for nativism than with the case for Locke's historical opponents.

First, we need to be clear as to the exact nature of the nativist's position. So far the meaning of the word 'innate' has only been explained in metaphorical terms, or by analogy with wax imprints and the like. 'Innate' literally means 'inborn', so that any innate human characteristic must at least be present from birth. To focus matters, let us suppose that what is at issue is the question of whether certain *cognitive states* are innate in human beings. I use the expression 'cognitive state' to embrace both knowledge and belief. It would be too narrow to discuss only the case of *knowledge*, since we should not presume that any innate cognitive state would have to constitute a *true* belief. Locke and his historical opponents of the seventeenth century naturally presumed this, but only because they assumed that any innate cognitive state would have to have a divine origin and therefore be veridical – God being no deceiver. Today we would naturally suppose, rather, that any innate cognitive state would have an evolutionary origin, and although it might seem unlikely that false beliefs could confer any adaptive advantage on human beings, this possibility cannot be ruled out – nor, indeed, can the possibility that some false innate beliefs might be the cognitive equivalent of the human appendix, useless but relatively harmless relics of other evolutionary developments. Of course, if there *are* innate cognitive states which have an evolutionary origin, then those states must in some sense be 'genetically programmed' in human beings. But it would be wrong to regard this as part of what it *means* to call a cognitive state innate, as opposed to part of a scientific theory purportedly *explaining* its innateness.

If certain cognitive states – that is, true or false beliefs – are innate in human beings, and thus possessed by them at birth, what evidence could we have for this? The beliefs in question will inevitably be *tacit* at that time, so that there is no question of their presence being evidenced by *linguistic* behaviour. But, of course, it is not only on the basis of their linguistic behaviour that we ascribe beliefs to other human beings, even when they do possess language. Quite generally, we ascribe beliefs to others in order to explain what we take to be their intentional behaviour, whether or not this is linguistic. This is because we explain people's intentional behaviour as being the product of their beliefs and desires. If I see someone cross a road and enter a bakery, I presume that he desires to buy some bread or cakes and believes that the shop will have them to sell. If I see someone take an umbrella with her as she leaves the house, I presume that she believes it may rain and desires not to get wet. Now, of course, we apply this form of belief–desire explanation even to the behaviour of young infants who cannot yet give voice to their beliefs and desires in language: if the baby crawls after a ball that has rolled behind a chair, we presume that it believes that the ball is there and desires to have it.

Could the nativist plausibly apply this model of belief-ascription in the case of supposedly innate beliefs? In principle, surely, yes. But the difficulty would lie in telling whether a belief in question really was innate or just acquired – learned – very early in the infant's career. Take, for example, one of Locke's favourite examples, the law of non-contradiction – which he, of course, supposes is *not* believed or in any sense understood by infants. Now, what sort of *non*-linguistic behaviour might constitute evidence for a belief in this law, the law that the same thing cannot 'both be and not be'? Well, perhaps evidence that a person holds this belief is provided by the fact that he does not attempt to perform contradictory actions at one and the same time – does not, for instance, attempt to open and close a door simultaneously. Here one might be tempted to protest that *the law itself* prevents the possibility of there being any such evidence, since it implies that a door cannot be both open and shut (= not open). But while it is true that the law prohibits the *success* of any attempt to perform contradictory actions, it does not prohibit the *attempt*: someone *could*, for instance, simultaneously push a door with one hand and pull it with the other. The fact that not even very young infants appear to attempt things like this might be taken to imply that they have a tacit grasp of the law, and refrain from the attempt because they *know* it is bound to fail. (Here it may be remarked that so-called 'split-brain' patients *have* been claimed to attempt to perform contradictory actions – though perhaps their case should be redescribed as one in which different hemispheres of the brain attempt to do conflicting things.)

However, the problem remains that, while the foregoing considerations may lend some credibility to the suggestion that even very young infants possess a belief in a principle like that of the law of non-contradiction, they do nothing to show that such a belief is *innate*, as opposed to just being acquired very early. Indeed, no amount of evidence that a belief is *possessed* at or soon after birth can, of itself, show that that belief is innate. What is additionally required is some consideration to the effect that the belief in question could not plausibly have been *acquired* or *learned*. (In a way, this is partly to concede a point made by Locke which we criticised in the previous section.) In the case of a belief in the law of non-contradiction, such a consideration might be this: that no one who *lacked* that belief would be capable of learning or being taught it. For if one is to learn that a certain proposition is true, one must presumably grasp, in the process, that that proposition is not also *false*, which is an application of the law of non-contradiction. Hence the truth of the law cannot itself be learned, because knowledge of it is a prerequisite of all successful learning. Perhaps the same applies to other fundamental principles of logic.

This sort of consideration – that knowledge of certain principles is a prerequisite of certain learning processes and therefore cannot be acquired by those processes – features prominently in modern nativist theories, the most famous of which is Noam Chomsky's theory of innate 'universal grammar' (see Chomsky 1972 and Fodor 1981). This is the theory that certain syntactical principles common to all natural human languages are genetically programmed in the language centre of the human brain, the argument being that human infants could not acquire their native tongue as quickly as they do by listening to the fragmented and imperfectly articulated conversation of their elders unless they already 'knew' certain elementary rules of linguistic structure.

Another sort of consideration which can be advanced in support of a claim that an early belief is innate rather than acquired is that the child has had no *opportunity* to acquire it. For instance, some developmental psychologists believe that children have certain innate cognitive structures concerning the spatial organisation of objects in three dimensions, reflected in their ability to make judgements of depth or to avoid approaching obstacles (see Bower 1989). The innateness of these beliefs can be tested by subjecting infants to circumstances in which they need to exploit such abilities *for the first time*. For example, a child which has never been exposed to heights may be tested on the so-called 'visual cliff' (a glass-covered pit, shallow at one end and deep at the other), to see whether it instinctively avoids the deep end and thus evinces an innate recognition of visual depth cues.

In the light of the preceding considerations, it seems plausible to contend that at least some components of human knowledge and belief – including, perhaps, elementary logical laws, certain structural rules of language and principles of spatial organisation – have an innate basis, explicable in terms of the evolutionary advantage such cognitive structures confer, in helping us to acquire other useful knowledge more quickly than we otherwise could (if, indeed, we could do so at all in their absence). But what would Locke have made of this contention? Would he have persisted in his resistance to nativism, even in its modern forms? I suspect not. For one thing, modern nativism completely severs the doctrine of innate ideas from any suggestion of divine origin, and for that reason there is no danger that a modern nativist claim may be used to imply the unquestionable truth of some favoured principle and to protect it from criticism by charges of impiety. Second, modern nativism is, queer though this may initially sound, not incompatible with empiricism, as I shall now try to explain.

There is a perennial danger of confusing the distinction between innate and acquired knowledge with the distinction between a priori and a posteriori knowledge. A priori knowledge is knowledge which is 'prior' to experience, but not in the sense that it is necessarily *possessed* before its owner has had any experience – only, rather, in the sense that in the case of a truth knowable a priori, a claim to know it does not depend for its justification upon any appeal to evidence supplied by experience. Thus, the arithmetical truth '2 + 5 = 7' is knowable a priori and yet it may still be the case that some or all people owe their knowledge of it to their experience of combining small groups of objects and counting them, and consequently that it is not innately known. Similarly, it is possible that a belief that is innate may depend for its truth as an item of knowledge upon circumstances whose obtaining can only be ascertained by recourse to empirical evidence. A creature might be born with a belief that a certain variety of toadstools is poisonous, but whether they *are* poisonous cannot be determined independently of experiment and observation. We must distinguish, then, between the question of what *caused* someone to possess a given belief and the question of how that belief might be *justified*. (A complication which we cannot go into here is that some modern epistemologists reject the traditional account of knowledge as justified true belief in favour of an account of it as belief caused by a reliable process.)

Now, if by 'empiricism' we mean the doctrine that all purport-edly scientific claims about the nature of the world require to be justi-fied by recourse to experimental or observational evidence – contrary to Descartes's relatively aprioristic view of the scientific enterprise – then it is clear that the claim that innate cognitive states exist may be regarded as a scientifically acceptable one according to the empiricist criterion. That is to say, it may be an *empirically warrantable fact* that there are innate cognitive states (as, for example, Chomsky would maintain).

Indeed, we can perhaps go even further in reconciling empiri-cism with the doctrine of innate ideas. For even if it is maintained that individual members of the human species are today born with certain innate cognitive states, which those individuals have therefore not acquired through their own experience, it may still be conceded that the 'experience' of earlier members of the species may have had a role to play in the evolutionary process whereby possession of those states came to be an inherited trait of their descendants. In that sense, even if 'empiricism' is construed as a doctrine concerning the *causes* of our cognitive states, nativism at an 'ontogenetic' level is compatible with empiricism at a 'phylogenetic' level (the levels of individual and species development respectively). Thus, for example, human infants today may have an innate recognitional capacity for visual depth cues because far back in our evolutionary history individuals better able to recognise such cues proved to be better adapted to their environment and were favoured by 'natural selection' on that account. If we treat 'experience' in the broadest sense as a transaction between an indi-vidual and its environment, we can say that such an evolutionary account of the origin of an innate cognitive state makes reference to the 'experience' of the predecessors of current possessors of the state (and does so without falling into the Lamarckian heresy of envisaging the inheritance of acquired characteristics). As such, this sort of account of the existence of 'innate ideas' is a wholly *naturalistic* one which is, to that extent, in the spirit of Locke's scientifically minded approach to the origins of human knowledge.

Finally, an acceptance of nativist claims in the account of the *causes* of our beliefs and concepts need not compromise Locke's analytic programme of attempting to show how all of our complex ideas are analysable in terms of simple components reflecting elements of human perceptual experience. We should thus distinguish – as Locke does not – between what might be called *genetic* empiricism (whether 'onto-' or 'phylo-') and *analytic* empiricism, the former concerned with how our beliefs and concepts are produced, the latter with their internal logical and semantic relationships to one another and to the contents of our experience. The contents of experience might provide the semantic basis of our conceptual repertoire even if our possession of that repertoire cannot be wholly explained in terms of our exposure to those contents.

We see, thus, that it is possible to identify at least three different brands of 'empiricism' – *scientific*, *genetic* and *analytic* – all mixed together in Locke's approach, but only the second of these is (and then only in one form) incompatible with nativism.

Chapter 3

Perception

Ideas and sense-perception

We saw at pp. 19–22 above that Locke uses the term 'idea' to refer to what in more recent writings are variously called *percepts*, or *sense data*, or *qualia*. It is evident that he considers that ideas in this sense are intimately involved in the processes of sense-perception whereby we see, hear, smell, taste and feel physical objects in our environment, and thereby come to acquire perceptual knowledge of their properties and relations. By no means all modern philosophers and psychologists would agree with this. According to one school of thought, perceiving an object is not at all like feeling a pain. Rather, perception is considered simply to be a mode of belief-acquisition, and while beliefs must indeed have meaningful propositional content – and thus involve 'ideas' in the sense of *concepts* – there is no reason to suppose that any element of *sensation* is literally involved in perception. I shall offer a defence of Locke's position in due course, but first we

35

need to be clearer about the precise role he assigns to ideas (= percepts) in perception.

Perhaps we can capture the basic form of Locke's theory of sense-perception by the following rudimentary schema:

1. Subject S perceives object O if and only if S has an idea I of O

where S is a person and O is an 'external' object, such as a ball or a tree. This schema is compatible with a variety of different interpretations of the details of Locke's theory, depending on how one explains its key elements. In particular, we need to consider what is involved in a subject's 'having an idea', what is involved in an idea's being 'of' a certain object, and how sense-perception differs from processes like memory and imagination (a question we shall examine more fully in Chapter 7). We also, crucially, need to examine the ontological status of ideas: what sort of things they are, if indeed they are 'things' in any sense at all.

One point that is immediately clear is that Locke is wedded to some form of *causal* theory of perception. Ideas, he says, are 'produced in us ... *by the operation of insensible particles on our Senses*' (2.18.13). In the case of sight, these will be particles of light (photons, as physicists now call them) impinging upon the retina of the eye, and thereby giving rise to activity in the optic nerves leading to the visual centres of the cerebral cortex. What happens then – the production of 'ideas' in the mind – is, Locke concedes, something of a mystery, but no more so than the mystery of how damage to a limb can give rise to a sensation of pain, with its subjective quality of intense unpleasantness.

Locke's advocacy of this sort of causal story may appear to commit him to a denial of what is known as 'direct' realism – the view that the 'immediate' objects of perception are ordinary physical objects like trees and rocks. But whether that is actually so depends on his view of the ontological status of ideas – whether they are 'objects' of some sort – and how the mind is related to them – whether it 'perceives' them. We shall see in later sections that on these matters Locke's views are open to more than one interpretation.

Another important point concerns Locke's conception of the relationship between perceptual experience and perceptual judgement. He appears to claim (2.9.8) that when we form a perceptual judgement concerning the properties of some perceived object, that judgement imposes an (unreflective) interpretation upon the ideas of sense produced in us by the object, very much in the way that interpretation is involved in judging what properties objects are depicted as possessing in a painted scene or photograph. How literally he wants us to take this analogy will again depend upon what exactly his view is of the nature of ideas. On the most simple-minded reading of the text, we might take him to be saying that ideas *are* just mental 'pictures' or 'images', which we scrutinise internally and interpret in various ways. But more sophisticated readings of the text are also possible, and make Locke's view much more defensible.

Here it is worth briefly mentioning the role of the *retinal* image in visual perception. The discovery of such images earlier in the seventeenth century had been a source of great fascination and debate – not least because these optical images, formed through the focusing of light from distant objects by the cornea and lens, are 'upside-down' (as in an astronomical telescope). Descartes (as he describes in his *Optics* of 1637) demonstrated the ability of the eye to produce such images – just in the way a camera does – by replacing the retina of a detached ox's eye with a translucent screen. One question immediately raised was this: how do we manage to see things 'the right way up', given that the 'pictures' which they produce at the back of the eye are inverted? The question seems to presuppose that we see 'external' things only *indirectly*, by looking at these pictures of them (rather as by looking at modern TV images). And it is tempting to suppose that Locke and other seventeenth-century philosophers conceived of visual 'ideas' as inner, mental analogues of these retinal images.

However, though the issue is too complex to be gone into here, I think that such a diagnosis is unwarranted. It will not do to criticise seventeenth-century philosophers as having been naively led to a supposedly incoherent 'imagist' theory of perception by their alleged misconception of the role of the newly discovered retinal images in visual perception. Imagist theories may indeed be open to criticism – as we shall discover in the next section – but they are not as blatantly untenable and confused as some of their modern critics have claimed them to be.

The traditional interpretation of Locke's view

Let us recall the schema we deployed in the previous section to characterise Locke's conception of the process of perception:

1. Subject *S* perceives object *O* if and only if *S* has an idea *I* of *O*.

According to one long-standing tradition of Locke commentary, perhaps deserving to be called the 'orthodox interpretation', the right-hand side of schema 1 should be understood in such a way that (a) an idea *I* is a mental *image* which (b) is *perceived* by the subject *S* and which (c) is both *caused by* the object *O* and *represents O* by way of *resemblance* with *O*. (For something approaching this view, see Aaron 1937, pp. 88ff.) Thus, 1 comes to be filled out more specifically in the following terms:

2. Subject *S* perceives object *O* if and only if *S* perceives a mental image *I* which is produced by an (appropriate) causal process originating in *O* and which represents *O* by way of resembling *O*.

In calling *I* a 'mental image', I am taking it to be some sort of *object*, with perceptible properties of its own, to which the subject *S* can stand in a genuine relationship, and more specifically a *perceptual* relationship. On this view, we literally *see* our visual ideas, and see them to possess various visible properties of colour and shape. Moreover, these visible properties (or some of them, anyway) *resemble*, to a greater or lesser degree, the visible properties of the 'external' objects which we see by the aid of the ideas they produce in us, enabling these ideas to represent the objects in much the same way as patches of paint on a canvas represent the objects depicted by the artist. On this interpretation, then, Locke is committed to a fully fledged version of the so-called 'representative theory of perception', or 'indirect realism'.

Having set up Locke in this fashion, many commentators then proceed to knock him down gleefully, pointing out all the supposed absurdities and difficulties of the theory that they have imputed to him. Let us consider what some of these alleged problems are, and whether they really are unanswerable, before we discuss whether or not Locke really did hold such a theory.

First of all, it may be protested that in saying, for instance, that one *sees* a tree by *seeing* a visual image of a tree, one has at best left the notion of seeing unexplained and at worst has embarked upon a vicious infinite regress. If one needs to see a visual image in order to see a tree, does one not by the same token need to see *another* visual image in order to see the first one, and so on *ad infinitum*? In a word: No. One might argue with as little cogency that anyone who claims that we need to see infra-red TV images in order to see things in the dark is committed to saying that we need to see *other* infra-red TV images in order to see the first ones. The point is that the circumstances which make it necessary for us to look at infra-red TV images in order to see certain things – namely, that the latter are *in the dark* – do not attend the infra-red TV images themselves. The 'imagist' must, in all charity, be construed as taking a comparable view of the relevant differences between mental images and 'external' objects. That is to say, he believes that there are cogent reasons for supposing that 'external' objects can only be seen 'indirectly' – reasons which do not apply in the case of visual images or ideas. (One such reason might be that we are subject to illusion and deception in our perception of external objects, but not in our perception of our own ideas – though how cogent a reason this would be is certainly open to question.)

Even so, the indirect realist is still faced with the lesser charge that, in 'explaining' what it is to perceive an 'external' object in terms of perceiving an 'inner' mental image caused by that object, he has really advanced our understanding of perception not at all, because he just helps himself to the very notion – of *perceiving* – that we desire to have explained. What *is* it to 'perceive' a mental image? If an account is offered that is identical in form to that offered in explanation of our perception of 'external' objects, then an infinite regress will indeed be under way. So some *alternative* account of what it is to 'perceive' is required in the case of mental images, and that then raises two further problems. First, this would imply that all perception verbs, like 'see' and 'hear', are systematically ambiguous, which may strike one as being both extravagant and implausible. Second, if an alternative account *can* be devised, why should it not be equally applicable to our perception of 'external' objects themselves, thus rendering the original account of our perception of these redundant? For instance, if it is said that to perceive a mental image is to be 'aware' or 'conscious' of it, can it not equally be said that we can in this sense 'perceive' *external* objects – for can one not be 'aware' or 'conscious' of something like a tree or a rock?

The obvious response for the 'indirect realist' to make to this last question is to say that we can only ever be *indirectly* aware of something like a tree, by virtue of being directly aware of some inner mental image of it. But then this just duplicates, in terms of the notion of *being aware*, the very issue we have been discussing in connection with the notion of *perceiving*. It looks as though the only way out of this apparent impasse for the indirect realist is to claim that there is a special, primitive and unanalysable notion of perception or awareness which applies exclusively to the relationship between a subject of experience and his or her own mental images or ideas. But perhaps that is not an illegitimate claim: after all, analysis may have to come to an end *somewhere* – some concepts may indeed be primitive and unanalysable, and maybe the only way in which we can discover that this is so in the case of a given concept is to find that we *cannot* analyse it further, and yet understand it perfectly adequately.

But there are other alleged problems for indirect realism. One is that it is supposed to give rise to scepticism, by interposing a 'veil' of ideas between us and 'external' objects, so that instead of providing an account of how we can come to know the properties of those objects through perception, it actually suggests that we *cannot* know them. If such objects are related to us merely as external *causes* of our ideas, what reason can we have to suppose anything definite about the nature of those objects? In particular, how can we know that their properties *resemble* those of our ideas in any respect? Indeed, does it even make sense to suppose that terms descriptive of ideas should also be applicable, univocally, to objects supposedly so different in kind from ideas – for instance, that both a visual image and an external object could be 'square', in the very same sense of the word? We shall return to some of these issues when we discuss the distinction between primary and secondary qualities (see pp. 53–9 below). For the time being, however, I just want to remark that I do not, in fact, believe that the 'indirect' realist is any *more* vulnerable to the threat of scepticism than is the 'direct' realist – a point which I shall explain further in the next section.

Yet another difficulty that is often raised for the indirect realist concerns the nature of the causal process supposedly leading to the production of mental images or ideas. How can a physical process, such as what Locke describes as 'the operation of insensible particles', give rise to something so apparently different in kind as a mental image? Locke himself seems to concede that there is an element of mystery in this, though he remarks (2.8.13) that there is no reason why God should not have so ordered things that ideas are 'annexed' to certain physical operations in a systematic way. The mention of 'God' here looks like a concession to anti-naturalism – an appeal, indeed, to a supernatural element in human make-up. But really it is only a concession that certain aspects of human psychology may have to be accepted as 'brute facts', not susceptible to further explanation – particularly certain aspects of human subjectivity (aspects of 'what it is like to be' a human being, in the memorable phrase of Thomas Nagel (1979)). And that may well have to be conceded by *anyone* who acknowledges the existence of a gulf between subjective aspects of conscious experience on the one hand and the impersonal, objective features of scientifically describable physical reality on the other. Thus, once again, it does not appear that this is a problem peculiar to indirect realism as such.

Is there anything *at all* especially problematical about indirect realism? Just this, I think: there is the problem of the ontological status of 'ideas' as this view conceives of them. It is a problem which also has a connection with the issue discussed earlier of the nature of the supposed relationship between a subject and his or her own ideas. The point is that the indirect realist takes ideas or images to be *objects*, or *entities*, or *things* of a special kind, which indeed *can* stand in a genuine *relationship* to the subject or mind that 'owns' them – such as the relationship of being perceived by that subject. Now, things that can stand in a genuine relationship to one another are normally – indeed, perhaps always and necessarily – logically independent of one another, in the sense that either could, logically (even if not naturally), exist in the absence of the other. Thus, for example, given two human beings related as father to son, although it is not naturally possible for the son to have existed in the absence of the father, nonetheless it appears *logically* possible that he should have done so, because these two people are, as Hume would put it, 'distinct and separable existences'. Now, the problem is that it simply does *not* appear to make sense to suppose that a given subject's 'ideas' could exist in the absence of that subject, either as free-floating and unattached ('unperceived') ideas or even as the ideas of *another* subject. In the same way, there could not be a pain which was not the pain of a particular person, nor could one person's pain have 'belonged' to another. The apparent logical incoherence of these suggestions indicates that there is something seriously wrong with the indirect realist's 'reification' of ideas as *things* of a peculiar sort. But if 'ideas' are *not* 'things', are they therefore *nothing at all* – that is, is the only alternative to treating them as the indirect realist does simply to deny their existence altogether? No: there is another much more attractive alternative, which we shall explore in the next section – an alternative which it is not altogether implausible to construe Locke himself as espousing.

An 'adverbialist' interpretation of Locke

Here I want to explore an alternative, 'adverbialist' reading of our original perception schema:

1. Subject *S* perceives object *O* if and only if *S* has an idea *I* of *O*.

The intention of this alternative reading is to avoid the *reification* of 'ideas' as *things* of some sort which stand in genuine relationships (of being perceived and being caused) to subjects and objects of perception. In order to explain the 'adverbialist' strategy, it may help to begin with its application to a quite different area of discourse, in which its appropriateness seems unquestionable.

Philosophers often allege, sometimes with good reason, that the syntax of ordinary language is misleading: in particular, Indo-European languages, of which English is an example, seem to be overburdened with nouns. (Other families of languages, such as Amerindian languages, appear to put more emphasis on verbs.) Consider, for instance, the following sentence:

a. John gave a broad grin.

Since the most typical use of a noun is to make reference to a *thing* of some sort, the surface syntax of a invites us to suppose that it states the existence of a relationship between one thing, John, and another, a 'grin', the latter being described by the adjective 'broad' as possessing a certain property. Compare

    b. John wore a broad hat

in which case the foregoing sort of relational analysis is perfectly appropriate. Hats *are* things of a certain sort, which possess certain properties and stand in genuine relationships to other things, such as people.

But despite the surface similarity between a and b, we do not, of course, imagine that such a relational analysis is really appropriate in the case of a. One way to make this clear is to point out that we are prepared to accept the following paraphrase of a as somehow more faithfully reflecting the state of affairs which it reports:

    c. John grinned broadly.

Here the noun 'grin' has been replaced by a verb, and the adjective 'broad' has been transformed into an adverb modifying that verb. At the same time, the original verb of a, 'gave', has disappeared without replacement, indicating that its role in a was purely syntactical – indeed, 'syncategorematic' (that is, devoid of independent semantic import). In short, the verb phrase 'gave a grin' as it appears in a has only the appearance of semantic structure – it is in fact just equivalent *en bloc* to the simple verb 'grinned' which appears in c.

Here one might be inclined to ask whether a similar grammatical transformation might not be applied to b. Clearly, as far as idiomatic English is concerned, it cannot. We cannot say something like

    d. John hatted broadly.

But could we not just *invent* a new verb, 'to hat', stipulating that '*x* hatted' means '*x* wore a hat'? Yes, we could, but it seems clear that this would *not* serve to show that the original verb of b, 'wore', has no genuinely independent semantic import. The point is that the verb 'to wear' expresses a relationship in which one thing can stand to things of many other different kinds: one can wear hats, shoes, coats, shirts – the list is endless (literally). Thus, if the strategy invoked in d were invoked quite generally to 'eliminate' all occurrences of the verb 'to wear' in English, the task would be an endless (potentially infinite) one. One would have to invent an open-ended list of new verbs, 'to hat', 'to shoe', 'to coat', and so on and on. This shows that there really is a relevant difference between the 'natural' paraphrase c of a and the 'cooked-up' paraphrase d of b. The difference reflects not just an arbitrary limitation in ordinary English vocabulary, but a deeper semantic – and ultimately ontological – distinction.

Armed with these reflections, let us return to the issue of the interpretation of schema 1, and in particular to the interpretation of the clause '*S* has an idea *I* of *O*'. We saw in the preceding section that what I called the 'traditional' interpretation of Locke's view envisaged him as regarding ideas as *things* bearing visible properties – such as colour and shape – and standing in genuine relationships to subjects (being *perceived* by them). Thus, on that view, a sentence like

e. John saw a red idea

could be regarded as grammatically well formed and interpretable at its syntactic face-value as expressing a genuinely relational proposition. Given, however, the metaphysical objections to the notion of ideas as things, it is obviously an attractive suggestion to apply the 'adverbialist' strategy to e, paraphrasing it as something like

f. John sensed redly.

(I shall explain in due course why 'sensed' rather than 'saw' is used in f.) In support of such a move, we might point to the fact that Locke himself clearly thinks of ideas as being in the same category as such sensations as *pains*, and observe that ordinary idiomatic English permits the paraphrase of

g. John felt a sharp pain in his side

by something like

h. John's side pained him sharply.

Now, of course, *neither* e *nor* f is a sentence of ordinary idiomatic English, but still we may be encouraged by the example of g and h to consider that if the vocabulary of 'ideas' *is* to be introduced into our language, it would be appropriate to apply the adverbialist strategy to it.

Such a move would imply that our original schema 1 ought to be filled out in something like the following way:

3. Subject S perceives object O if and only if S senses I-ly and S's sensing I-ly is appropriately caused by O.

It will be noted that I have used the verb 'sense', rather than 'perceive', on the right-hand side of 3. This is because it is an implication of the adverbialist approach that perceiving is genuinely *relational* in nature, so that we need a new, *intransitive* verb to express what was 'traditionally' treated as a relationship between a subject and an idea. We can stipulate that 'sense' is to be construed in this way.

What schema 3 brings out is that, on this interpretation, the language of 'ideas' is meant *not* to talk about a class of *entities* with various sensible properties of colour and shape, and so forth, but rather to talk about the *modes* or *manners* in which experiencing subjects are sensibly affected by perceptible objects like tables and rocks. On this view, our recourse to *nouns* and *adjectives* in the language of ideas, instead of *verbs* and *adverbs*, is just due to an inconvenient syntactical legacy of Indo-European languages. (For further debate, see Jackson 1977, pp. 63ff., and Tye 1989.)

Suppose we accept the adverbialist strategy as being the philosophically correct one to adopt: there is still the question of whether it is in fact *Locke's* strategy, and there is also the question of what, if any, advantages it has over the more traditional imagist (or 'act–object') approach.

As to the first question, my view is that it is probably fruitless to speculate whether Locke was 'really' an act–object theorist or an adverbialist, because I do not think that he was alive to the issue – unlike the later Berkeley, who does seem to have been alive to it, eventually favouring an act–object approach despite an early flirtation with the view that ideas are 'manners of the existence of persons' (*Philosophical Commentaries*, B24). One leading Locke scholar who seems to regard Locke as a proto-adverbialist is John Yolton, who remarks, for instance, that, for Locke

Having visual images *is* seeing objects, under specific conditions. The way of ideas is Locke's method of recognising the mental features of seeing. It does not place the perceiver in some vale of ideas forever trying to break out into the world of physical objects. (Yolton 1970, p. 132)

Yolton goes on to remark: 'I see no evidence in the *Essay* that Locke thought of ideas as entities' (p. 134). It is certainly true – as we shall see in Chapter 8 (pp. 175–80) – that Locke did not consider that his theory of perception has the sceptical implications that critics of the traditional, imagist interpretation of it claim it to have. But that need not imply that Locke did *not* hold an imagist view, even if we do not wish to impugn Locke's philosophical intelligence, because – as I have already mentioned – I do not in fact believe that the imagist or act–object approach is inherently more vulnerable to sceptical problems than is the adverbialist approach.

This brings us directly to the second question raised a moment ago, concerning the relative merits of the two approaches. I have already stated that I consider the adverbialist approach to be *ontologically* superior: it does away with what would otherwise appear to be a queer class of entities, and if it succeeds in doing this without loss of explanatory power then it can fairly appeal to Occam's razor in its support (to the principle, that is, that we should not 'multiply entities beyond necessity'). But I do not, as I say, believe that the adverbialist approach has any *epistemological* advantage over the act–object approach. It is tempting to suppose otherwise because of the familiar rhetoric about the veil (or, as Yolton has it, the 'vale') of ideas, suggesting that ideas, on the imagist conception, almost literally form a curtain screening the subject off from the world of 'external' objects. But the force of this rhetoric turns merely on its choice of metaphor. One might just as well have used the metaphor of a *window* or of a *bridge*, giving the subject *access* to the world of outer objects. Metaphors aside, the crucial point is that even if an adverbialist, direct-realist approach is taken, according to which the immediate objects of perception are always 'external' objects like rocks and trees, no guarantee is thereby provided that the subject ever *does* enter into such perceptual relationships with such objects. For scepticism trades on the fact that the subject could, apparently, be in the same internal experiential state *whether or not* that state involves the presence of 'outer' objects. And this consideration, for what it is worth, carries exactly the same weight whether we analyse that experiential state adverbially (as the subject's sensing in a certain manner) or in an act–object way (as the subject's perceiving a certain image or sense-datum).

There is one other issue concerning the differences between the two approaches which deserves some mention here. I described the imagist approach of the preceding section as endorsing a *representative* theory of perception, in which representation is at least partly achieved by *resemblances* between the properties of ideas and the properties of 'external' objects. It might seem that this aspect of the act–object approach could have no counterpart in the adverbialist approach (and, indeed, I included no such explicit counterpart in schema 3), because the latter has done away with the very entities whose properties were supposed to 'resemble' those of things like trees and rocks. In fact, however, we shall see below (pp. 59–65) that a form of representationalism plausibly *is* implied by the adverbialist approach, and even some notion of 'resemblance' is not wholly out of place. Just because we espouse a strategy of replacing adjectives by adverbs in our characterisation of the qualitative content of sensory experience, this does not mean that we cannot see semantic connections between ways of characterising that content and ways of describing 'external' objects. After all, having paraphrased 'John gave a broad grin' as 'John grinned broadly', we do not have to abandon any thought of a connection in meaning between the adverb 'broadly' as it is used to characterise an action of grinning and the adjective 'broad' as it is used to describe a hat – despite the deep ontological differences between actions and objects.

Locke's account of secondary qualities as powers

In distinguishing between 'primary' and 'secondary' qualities of physical objects, Locke was following an already well-established tradition adopted by other seventeenth-century philosophers and scientists, including Descartes, Newton and Boyle. There was, however, some disagreement as to precisely how the distinction should be defined, and consequently also some disagreement as to precisely which qualities fell into which category. Locke considered that the primary qualities of a body were those that were 'inseparable' from it (2.8.9), and in this he seems to agree with Isaac Newton (1686) – who, for instance, regarded what we should now call *mass* as a primary quality, but not *weight* (because a massive object becomes weightless in the absence of a gravitational field). A closely related notion is that the primary qualities of a body are its *intrinsic* and *non-relational* properties – those which it could in principle possess even in the absence of any other body (a suggestion which Robert Boyle (1666) made vivid by contemplating the case of a single material atom existing alone in the void). Another suggestion, naturally associated with the name of René Descartes, is that the primary qualities are those which a physical body possesses purely by virtue of being *material* – in other words (at least on Cartesian principles), by virtue of being spatially *extended*. Thus the primary qualities would comprise extension and its 'modes' – shape, size, velocity, and so forth – in short, the geometrical and kinematic properties of objects.

All of these suggestions, coupled with the presumption of seventeenth-century science that physical explanation is primarily *mechanical* explanation – explanation in terms of motion and impact – point to the idea that the primary qualities are the objective, 'scientific' properties of physical objects, the only ones that ultimately need to be appealed to in order to explain the law-governed causal interactions of bodies of whatever sort, from atoms to stars. This conception of the status of the primary qualities is reflected also in Locke's thesis – which we shall examine more closely in the next section – that the primary qualities are those of which our corresponding ideas are *resemblances*, the implication being that in their case the gap between appearance and reality is much smaller than in the case of the more subjective secondary qualities of colour, taste and smell.

I remarked that different seventeenth-century authors included different properties in their lists of primary qualities, and certainly there are some oddities in the list Locke provides: 'Solidity, Extension, Figure, Motion, or Rest, and Number' (2.8.9), to which he elsewhere adds 'Bulk' and 'Texture' (2.8.10). The notion that *number* is a 'quality' or 'property' of objects, whether primary or secondary, is peculiar, and certainly one which we would reject today. Again, solidity, while clearly a property of physical objects, is not one that indisputably qualifies as primary by the criteria of Locke and other contemporary authors. After all, a 'solid' object can be made liquid or gaseous by the application of heat, so the solidity of an object, at least in the ordinary sense of the term, is not 'inseparable' from it. It is true that Locke's 'solidity' is probably better construed as meaning something more like 'impenetrability' – but spelling out an acceptable sense in which a *gas*, say, is 'impenetrable' is no easy matter. Be that as it may, it seems that there is a sufficiently clear core of qualities agreed by all parties to the distinction to count as 'primary', and likewise sufficient agreement over which qualities are paradigmatically 'secondary'. The former are qualities like shape, size, mass and velocity, the latter ones like colour, smell and taste. In the next section I shall examine some objections to *any* attempt to draw a principled distinction between two such classes of qualities, but for the time being I shall accept the distinction uncritically and concentrate on examining Locke's theory of the nature of the secondary qualities.

These secondary qualities, Locke tells us, are 'Powers to produce various Sensations in us' (2.8.10) – moreover, they are 'nothing but' such powers. Take the example of a colour quality, such as redness. We are inclined to think of redness as a *surface* property of an object (in the case of a red object with a matt surface, at least, as opposed to one with a shiny surface, or one which glows red). Indeed, we are almost inclined to think of redness as a kind of *stuff*, spread thinly over an object's surface (or perhaps suffused throughout the object, in the case of an object made of homogeneously red material). Our very language encourages this view, or perhaps just reflects it. 'Red' is, grammatically, what the linguists call a *mass term*: we speak of 'some red' and 'more red' rather as we speak of 'some butter' and 'more butter'. Now, this natural and unphilosophical way of thinking about a quality like redness goes comfortably hand-in-hand with a view of perception which is sometimes called 'naive realism' (not to be equated with 'direct realism', in the sense of the latter discussed in the previous section). Naive realism is not so much a theory of perception as an absence of a theory: it involves a tacit assumption that the perceived qualities of physical objects are in the objects *just in the way they appear to be*, so that there is, in effect, no 'gap' between appearance and reality.

Now, when Locke affirms that secondary qualities are 'nothing but' powers in objects to produce various sensations – or ideas – in us, he is implicitly repudiating naive realism and the pre-reflective notion that a colour property like redness is 'on' the surface of an object just in the way it appears to be. But let us be clear also that Locke is *not* denying that redness really is a quality or property of the perceived object: he is just saying that this quality, *as it is in the object*, is a 'power' (or, as we would now call it, a 'disposition'), whose nature is not to be confused with that of the subjective idea or sensation of 'redness' which we typically enjoy upon being confronted with red objects. Rather, the nature of that power is ultimately to be described in terms of the *primary* qualities of the particles composing an object's surface, for it is these, Locke supposes, that confer upon that object the power to cause sensations of redness in us.

We are now in a position to venture on Locke's behalf an explicit account of what constitutes the secondary quality of redness in a physical object, as follows:

R. x is red = x possesses the power (disposition), by virtue of the primary qualities of its microstructural parts, to produce in us (or, more properly, to produce in a normal human percipient in standard conditions of vision) an idea or sensation of red.

A number of points about R call for immediate comment. First of all, one might be tempted to object that R is *circular*, because the very word 'red' occurs on the right-hand side of the identity sign as well as on the left. But that would, I think, be a mistake. For R should not be construed as a purported *definition* of the word 'red': Locke clearly regards the word 'red' as undefinable, because our *idea* of red is a simple one, and the function of the word 'red' is to operate as a sign of this idea (a view we shall explore more fully in Chapter 7). Indeed, Locke does not consider that anyone who has not enjoyed the experience of redness can really understand the word 'red' at all, as he makes vivid by his memorable anecdote concerning the blind man who, asked what he thought scarlet was like, allegedly answered that he thought it was like the sound of a trumpet (3.4.11)! Since 'red', on Locke's view, is undefinable, R must be construed as telling us something quite other than what that word signifies: it must be construed as telling us what *constitutes* redness in a physical object, that is, what it is about a physical object that makes it one to which the term 'red' is correctly applicable.

From this it does indeed seem to follow that, where R speaks of 'an idea or sensation *of red*', this had better not be construed as equivalent to 'a *red* idea or sensation', at least if 'red' in its latter occurrence were thought to be synonymous with 'red' as it appears on the left-hand side of R, in the expression '*x* is red'. For it is sufficiently clear that, by Locke's own theory, an *idea* could not *be red* in the way that a *physical object* is red according to principle R. For an *idea* has no microstructural parts with primary qualities; nor does an *idea* have a power to produce sensations in us – rather, it *is* a sensation in us. It must be confessed that these considerations appear to create a certain amount of tension in Locke's account, because it looks as though, on that account, 'red' in its most basic sense describes a quality of our *ideas* or *sensations*, and yet R seemed designed to tell us when the word 'red' – as it is ordinarily used – is correctly applicable *to a physical object*. It seems to follow that the ordinary use of the word cannot properly involve an application of it in its most basic sense. But perhaps it could be said on Locke's behalf that this correctly reflects the confusion that is involved in the ordinary speaker's assumption of naive realism. Words whose most basic senses derive from qualities of our sensations are ordinarily *applied* (in those very senses) in descriptions of physical objects.

Maybe the best way to handle this apparent difficulty is to construe R as telling us how to interpret the 'is' of predication appearing in '*x* is red', when *x* is a physical object: it tells us that that apparently simple verb is to be unpacked in terms of the complicated verb-phrase standing between '*x*' and 'red' on the right-hand side of R, while 'red' itself has the same primitive and unanalysable meaning in both of its occurrences in R. In this way we can avoid both any charge of circularity and any pressure to treat colour words as systematically ambiguous, holding both that their sense derives from the character of our colour sensations and yet that colours can still coherently be predicated of 'external' objects, given the proper understanding of what such 'predication' amounts to.

It will be noticed that I have included in R, on Locke's behalf, a reference to 'normal' percipients and 'standard' conditions – because, obviously, a red object will not *appear* red (that is, produce in an observer a sensation 'of red') if, say, the observer is red–green colour-blind, or if the object is illuminated by blue light. Spelling out what is 'normal' and 'standard' is a notoriously difficult matter, and some philosophers believe that it simply cannot coherently be done (see Hardin 1988, pp. 67ff.). But the alternative would be to have to deviate extensively from our customary practices of colour ascription, and say, for instance, that an object which *is* red in ordinary sunlight changes to being black in blue light (since that is what it looks like). In fact we do not talk as though things can change their colours as easily as this: we say, rather, that a red object *appears to be* (not *is*) black in blue light, which implies that there are only certain select conditions in which it appears to be the colour that it really is.

Now, it has to be acknowledged that Locke himself was ambivalent about some of these matters, and perhaps even a little confused. For example, at one point he asks: 'Can any one think . . . that those *Ideas* of whiteness and redness, are really in [a body] in the light, when 'tis plain *it has no colour in the dark?*' (2.8.19). Here Locke seems to be confusing a repudiation of naive realism about colours (the thought that redness *as it characterises our visual sensations* is literally 'in' an external object) with a mistaken rejection of the stability of colour ascriptions (mistaken, that is, on the terms of his own theory of the latter). For if, as Locke maintains, redness *as it is in the object* is merely a *disposition* to produce certain sensations in us in appropriate circumstances, then we have no reason to *deny* that an object is red in this sense just because the appropriate circumstances do not obtain (for instance, if the object is 'in the dark'). One could with as little reason say that a grain of salt ceases to be water-soluble when it is removed from contact with water.

Locke's ambivalence about this is illustrated in another passage where, likening our ideas or sensations of colour to those of sickness or pain, he remarks that secondary qualities '*are no more really in* [bodies] *than Sickness or Pain is*. . . . Take away the Sensation of them . . . and [they] are reduced to their Causes' (2.8.17). These 'causes' are the *powers* or *dispositions* which bodies have to produce sensations of colour and the like in us – and the point is that Locke is ambivalent over the issue of whether the mere *possession* of these powers warrants ascriptions of colour to the objects possessing them, or whether we should say that the objects are 'really' coloured (to the extent that we can say this at all) only when those powers are *actually being manifested* by the production of the appropriate sensations in an observer. The account of colour ascription embodied in R appears to be a tenable one, but Locke himself, though suggesting such an account, does not always follow through its implications.

Berkeley's critique of the distinction between primary and secondary qualities

Writing some quarter of a century after the first appearance of the *Essay*, George Berkeley was to launch a vigorous and penetrating attack on Locke's philosophy of perception and his theory of the external world as a realm of material objects existing independently of the human mind and endowed with the scientific (because mechanical) primary qualities of mass, shape, size and motion. Berkeley's ultimate motive in attacking a position that had become the prevailing orthodoxy of the scientific and philosophical community of the early eighteenth century was his fear that it would provide a breeding-ground for atheism, scepticism and immorality, as it marginalised the role of divine power in sustaining and controlling the natural order by treating the physical world as nothing more than an insensate, unintelligent machine. Berkeley believed that the weakest point in this whole philosophical edifice was the very notion of *matter*, conceived of as some sort of mind-independent stuff adequately characterisable in terms of the so-called primary qualities alone. For it does seem to be an implication of Locke's distinction between primary and secondary qualities that a complete description of the physical world in terms of the primary qualities of its constituent bodies would be exhaustive, in the sense that it would leave nothing out except a description of the effects of those bodies on the minds of perceivers.

On Locke's view, it seems, there is nothing *more* to a body's possession of the various secondary qualities of colour, taste, smell, and so forth, than its possession of microstructural parts with primary qualities apt to produce certain appropriate sensations in us. But this implies that it must at least *make sense* to describe a physical object – such as, perhaps, a material atom – solely in terms of its primary qualities. Indeed, it seems to be implied that the ultimate constituents of physical objects – atoms themselves – *can only have* the primary qualities (since they have, *ex hypothesi*, no microstructural parts upon whose primary qualities any secondary qualities of those atoms could supervene). The material atoms of Locke's physical world must be possessed *only* of mass, shape, size and motion, and be devoid of colour, taste, warmth and smell.

Now it was Berkeley's great insight to see that there is a profound difficulty with this conception of physical reality – a difficulty which still afflicts the scientific materialism which is at least tacitly adopted by many philosophers and scientists today. The difficulty is indicated early on in Berkeley's *Principles of Human Knowledge* (I, 10). How can we even *conceive* of an object as possessing *only* such properties as mass, shape, size and motion? When we think of a certain object as possessing certain boundaries which define its shape and size and help to determine its path through space as it moves, we have to think of those boundaries as marked out in some way: some quality or property must serve to differentiate what falls within the boundary from what falls outside it, or else there is no determinate sense in which we are given a 'boundary' at all. Thus, we might envisage the interior of the boundary as being filled out by a certain *colour*, different from the colour of the exterior. We cannot, *pace* Descartes, characterise physical objects purely in terms of extension and its 'modes' – we require also the conception of some *intensive* quality (one which can vary in *degree* or *magnitude*, as a colour can vary in brightness or hue) which serves to differentiate the various extended parts of different bodies. Otherwise, no distinction can be made between a world of moving bodies with determinate shapes and sizes and a world consisting just of empty space. But none of the traditional primary qualities appears to be apt to occupy this role of providing intensive magnitude.

Here it may be replied that there is after all a candidate for this role – Locke's 'bulk', or its modern counterpart (if that is what it is), *mass*. But there is a grave difficulty in appealing to this, which is that the notion of mass, and related notions such as that of ability to resist penetration, are *dispositional* and *relational* in character. Thus

Newtonian inertial mass is definable in terms of a body's disposition to accelerate under the action of a force, in accordance with Newton's Second Law of Motion: the less a body accelerates under the action of a given force, the more massive it is (and this provides us with a measure of the *magnitude* of its mass). But the trouble is that the applicability of any such definition presupposes that we already have an adequate conception of what constitutes a *body*, and this is precisely what is now at issue. If all we know about 'bodies' is that they are *massive* objects with shape, size and motion, it helps us not at all to be told that mass is a dispositional property which *a body* has to accelerate at a given rate under the action of a given force. (The problem is further compounded by the fact that the notion of a *force* is correlatively defined in terms of its capacity to induce acceleration in a massive object.) Similarly, if, instead of 'bulk', 'solidity' is appealed to and explained in terms of an object's tendency to resist penetration *by another body*, no progress has yet been made in characterising the nature of bodies beyond ascribing to them the purely geometrical and kinematic properties of shape, size and motion.

Berkeley's contention, then, is that the *ontological* distinction that Locke wishes to make between primary and secondary qualities, with the former alone constituting the 'really real' properties of physical objects, is quite untenable. In this he seems to have quite a persuasive argument. The colourless, odourless, tasteless 'objective' world of science – the physical world supposedly 'as it is in itself' – does indeed seem to be an unintelligible abstraction from the world of human experience.

Berkeley has in addition another forceful objection to the way Locke characterises the primary/secondary distinction, this time focusing on Locke's thesis that there is a 'resemblance' between primary qualities and our ideas of them which is absent in the case of the secondary qualities and their corresponding ideas. More than once Berkeley pronounces his fundamental principle that 'an idea can be like nothing but an idea' (1975, p. 79) – the implication being that it is just unintelligible to suppose, as Locke seems to, that things as fundamentally different in nature as a lump of matter on the one hand and a mental image on the other could have a predicate like 'square' applied univocally to both of them. But if it is meaningless to talk of ideas and material objects sharing predicates, it seems to follow that they cannot meaningfully be said to resemble each other – and consequently Locke's claim that secondary qualities are distinctive inasmuch as the ideas we have of them do *not* resemble them turns out, after all, to capture not any special feature of the qualities in question, but one which would have to apply equally in the case of primary qualities.

On Locke's behalf it may be urged that a picture may 'resemble' the object it depicts without literally sharing any of the same predicates. A picture of a tree may be a 'good likeness' even though the tree is large, rough and three-dimensional, whereas the picture is small, smooth and flat. (Let us ignore the similarities in *colour*, since Locke precisely wants to deny resemblances in this respect between objects and ideas.) But there are problems with this defence. First of all, pictures and depicted objects do at least have in common that they are *spatially extended* things, even if they differ in their dimensionality – whereas Berkeley would want to say that ideas and Lockean material objects could not be alike even to this extent. Second, the reason why a picture can be a good likeness of something such as a tree is that, in suitable viewing circumstances, seeing the picture involves an experience quite similar to that involved in seeing a tree; but that presupposes that one can indeed *see* a tree independently of seeing a picture of it, and compare the two experiences – whereas, of course, Locke's theory of perception does not countenance the possibility of our experiencing material objects independently of experiencing ideas, and comparing the two cases. So a 'picture' theory of resemblance is of little or no use to Locke in explaining what he means in claiming that our ideas of primary qualities 'resemble' those qualities.

If we wish to defend Locke's resemblance thesis concerning the primary qualities and our ideas of them, we need to tackle head-on Berkeley's 'likeness principle', as we may call it. Berkeley does not explain what makes that principle true, but it seems to rest upon a deeper principle that items belonging to different ontological categories cannot share the same predicates univocally. Perhaps it is an early articulation of the notion of a 'category mistake', made famous by Gilbert Ryle (1949, ch. 1). And it has some plausibility. For example, it would be absurd to think that a *number* could be 'even' in precisely the same sense that a *surface* can be even, or that a *sea* can be 'angry' in the same sense that a *person* can. At most one can speak of *analogy* in these cases. But it does not appear that analogy is what Locke has in mind in speaking of resemblances between ideas and objects. Moreover, in order to understand an analogy we need to understand something about *both* of the types of things that the analogy concerns – both seas and persons, for instance. It is hard to see how we could understand something *only* by analogy. But our ideas of the primary qualities are precisely what, by Locke's account, are supposed to form the basis of our understanding of the nature of material objects – we have nothing else to go on, and therefore no basis for framing *analogies* between ideas and objects independently of the very ideas in question.

The solution, I believe, is simply to deny the supposed incoherence of cross-categorial predication, at least in some cases. Some sorts of predicates are 'topic-neutral', notably logico-mathematical ones. These may loosely be called *structural* descriptions. And then the point is that structures in radically different domains can sometimes bear relationships of isomorphism (sameness of form) to one another. For example, the structure exhibited in the order of the natural numbers, 1, 2, 3, . . ., can be seen reflected in a sequence of physical events, such as successive risings of the sun. Hence we can use that number sequence to represent the days of the month. Again (to use an example deployed by Bertrand Russell (1959b, p. 19)), there is a structural isomorphism between the pattern of grooves in a gramophone record and the pattern of sounds produced when the record is played – and between this and the pattern of marks on a written musical score. What can coherently be claimed, then, is that certain *structural isomorphisms* obtain between our ideas of the primary qualities and those qualities themselves. I shall discuss this suggestion more fully in the next section, where we shall see that it is tenable even on an 'adverbialist' account of the ontological status of 'ideas'. It is no accident, however, that the properties which should turn out to be likely candidates for possessing 'resemblances' with ideas in this structural sense are precisely the *geometrical* and *kinematic* properties of objects – for these are the properties whose description most intimately involves logico-mathematical terminology.

An interesting issue related to Locke's resemblance thesis is worth mentioning to conclude this section. This is what has become known as *Molyneux's Question*, posed to Locke by one of his many learned correspondents, the Irishman William Molyneux. Locke reports the question as follows:

> Suppose a Man born blind . . . and taught by his touch to distinguish between a Cube, and a Sphere . . . [is] then . . . made to see. [Mr Molyneux asks] Whether by his sight . . . he could now distinguish them, and tell, which is the Globe, which the Cube. . . . To which the acute and judicious Proposer answers: Not. (2.9.20)

The relevance of this question to the resemblance thesis is that it seems that a further distinction between primary and secondary qualities not mentioned so far is that the former, but not the latter, are perceptible by more than one sense modality. One can both *see* and *feel* an object's shape, but only *see* its colour, *feel* its warmth, *smell* its odour, and so on. But if our ideas of the primary qualities resemble those qualities, one would suppose it to follow that ideas from different sense modalities of the *same* primary quality would resemble *each other*, and consequently that a congenitally blind man newly made to see could discern a resemblance between his new *visual* idea of a cube and his old *tactile* idea of it, enabling him to distinguish the former from his new visual idea of a *sphere*, and thus to tell cubes and spheres apart by sight without further training. Yet Locke, as we see, agrees with Molyneux that we should *not* expect this result, which may appear to be inconsistent of him.

Leibniz, addressing this issue in the *New Essays* (1981, pp. 135 ff.), supposed that the blind man ought indeed to be able to distinguish the visual ideas of a cube and a sphere by means of their different properties of symmetry (a cube – seen face-on, at any rate – *appears visually* to have two distinguished axes of symmetry, unlike a sphere, and this would seem to correspond with a similar formal feature of the way a cube *feels tactilely*). However, the problem is complicated not only by the involvement of three-dimensionality and perspective (the latter phenomenon being entirely unfamiliar to the blind, at least in ordinary circumstances) but also by the apparent physiological impossibility of settling the answer empirically. For the development of the human visual system depends upon the creation of appropriate neural connections very early in life and requires the proper functioning of the eye at that stage, so that even if an operation is performed to restore that function at a later date (for example, by cataract removal), it will be too late to enable the patient to see. Such investigations as have been done on people whose sight has been restored some years after losing it in early childhood appear to be inconclusive (see Morgan 1977).

In defence of a moderate representationalism

Though contrary to mainstream philosophical opinion at present, a theory of perception along broadly Lockean lines is, I think, correct. The sort of theory I have in mind will be (a) a causal theory, (b) a 'representative' theory (in a sense I shall explain) and (c) a 'direct-realist' theory. Many present-day philosophers would suppose that such a combination of features is impossible, but properly interpreted they are not in fact incompatible. I also think that a theory with these features could be attributed to Locke, at least on an 'adverbialist' interpretation of his talk about 'ideas' (see pp. 42–7 above). But in this section I shall be concerned not so much with Lockean exegesis as with a presentation and defence of the sort of theory I have in mind (see further Lowe 1992).

It seems to me that any theory of perception that is to respect the known scientific facts of human physiology and the laws of physics must be a *causal* theory. (For present purposes, thus, I am assuming that 'realism', as opposed to 'idealism', concerning the 'external world' is correct: it is not my business here to contend with Berkeley's arguments against the existence of matter.) By a causal theory of perception I mean one which maintains that for a subject to *perceive* an object (a physical object, that is) it is at least necessary that that subject should enjoy some appropriate sort of *perceptual experience* which is *caused* in an appropriate sort of way by a process originating in the object perceived – as, for example, *seeing* an object involves enjoying a visual experience caused (typically) by light reflected or emitted by the object entering the eye and giving rise to a suitable pattern of neural activity in the optic nerve and the visual centres of the cerebral cortex. (It is necessary to specify that the perceptual experience be caused in an 'appropriate sort of way' in order to exclude various types of 'deviant' causal chain which would appear to be incompatible with genuine cases of perception: for example, a case in which a subject has a 'hallucinatory' experience as of seeing a dagger which is accidentally triggered off by a chain of events in which just such a dagger is involved. Defining what constitutes 'deviance' in a causal chain is a contentious matter, but I shall set aside this problem here.)

It is crucial to a causal theory of perception that one be able to give some account of the key notion of a 'perceptual experience' as a kind of mental state which can, in principle, occur even in the absence of its typical perceptual causes. The possibility – and, indeed, the actual occurrence – of seemingly veridical hallucinatory states (as, for instance, in the phenomenon of so-called 'lucid dreaming') appears to confirm that such an account should in principle be available. (Some modern philosophers deny that such an account is possible, claiming that one cannot 'abstract' from any perceptual process an 'end state' – a state of 'perceptual experience' – which is of a type common *both* to such a process *and* to such 'non-veridical' processes as hallucination. But I shall assume that they are mistaken in this.)

As to the *nature* of perceptual experiences, I should say that they have two key features: (a) they are 'representational' or 'intentional' states, and (b) they are 'qualitative' states. By a I mean that a perceptual experience always represents – or, better, *presents* – the environment of the subject as *being some way*: for example, a visual experience may present the subject's environment as containing a red book lying on a black table directly in front of the subject. By b I mean that a perceptual experience always *seems some way* to the subject – that, as Nagel (1979) puts it, there is always 'something it is like' to have the experience. Thus, there is 'something it is like' to have a visual experience as of seeing a red book lying on a black table directly in front of one – and because of this one can *imagine* what having such an experience would be like even if one has not actually had it. By contrast, there is nothing distinctive 'it is like' to *believe* that a red book is lying on a black table directly in front of one: beliefs, although 'intentional' states (a belief is always a belief *that* such-and-such is the case), are not qualitative states.

Now, I would say that perceptual experiences are qualitative states because they involve qualia – that is, in Locke's terminology, *ideas* (in one of the senses of that term explained at pp. 19–22 above). But I would prefer to understand talk of qualia or ideas in an 'adverbialist' way, rather than in an 'act–object' or 'imagist' way. Qualia are not *things* that we encounter in states of perceptual experience – rather, they are characteristics of those very states, and thus *ways* in which our experiences are modified, or differ from one another 'qualitatively'. If we use nouns to talk about qualia, that is just because the syntax of Indo-European languages favours that way of talking, and has no ontological significance. *Examples* of qualia would be the qualitative features of visual experience characteristic of, say, experiences of seeing *red* objects, or *black* objects, or objects lying *adjacent* to one another. In ordinary language, our main resource for talking about such features of experience lies in the use of words like 'look' and 'appear'. Thus, when I say that a red book *looks* black when seen in blue light, I am adverting to a distinctive qualitative feature of visual experience in these circumstances – a feature which *normally* attaches to our visual experiences of black things. Just as there are visual qualia corresponding to the colour properties of seen objects, so there are qualia corresponding to their geometrical properties and spatial relations to one another (properties like shape, and relations like adjacency).

It will be recalled that I declared the theory I wish to defend to be a 'direct-realist' theory of perception. What I mean by 'direct realism' in this context is a position which (a) affirms that we do perceive real physical objects existing independently of us (contrary to the claim of Berkeleian idealism), but (b) denies that we only perceive these 'indirectly' by virtue of perceiving private, 'inner', mental objects of some sort, such as mental images. My commitment to b follows, of course, from my adherence to the 'adverbialist' approach to qualia. By my account, we do not *perceive* (or otherwise stand in any genuine relation to) our qualia, and so *a fortiori* do not perceive 'external' objects *by* perceiving qualia corresponding to, or caused by, them. Our qualia are just qualitative features of the perceptual experiences we enjoy when we perceive the only sorts of objects we ever do perceive, namely, 'external', physical objects (though sometimes, it is true, these objects will not *literally* be external – they may be inside our own bodies). As for a, I have already declared my commitment to realism.

Thus far I have explained in what sense I wish to defend a theory of perception that is both a *causal* theory and a *direct-realist* theory – and have also, I hope, done something to vindicate the espousal of these features in a theory of perception. It remains only for me to explain in what sense my favoured theory is a *representative* theory, and how this feature of it may be justified. This to many will appear the most difficult task. First of all I need to explain the difference between a *representative* theory of perception and a *representational* theory of perception.

Any theory of perception which accepts, as I do, that perceptual experiences are 'representational' or 'intentional' states (states with *propositional* content, for instance) can be accounted a 'representational' theory of perception in the broadest sense of that term. I suppose that almost every modern theory of perception, whether framed by psychologists or by philosophers, will be 'representational' in this sense. As for the expression '*representative* theory of perception', this has traditionally been used to denote what I have been calling 'indirect realism' – that is, the view that we perceive 'external' objects only indirectly by perceiving (or otherwise being related to) 'inner' mental objects such as images or 'sense-data', these latter objects functioning as 'representatives' for the 'external' objects (rather, perhaps, in the way in which a Member of Parliament is a 'representative' for his or her constituents). It is a further ingredient of this traditional view that the images or sense-data *represent* 'external' objects at least partly by way of *resemblance* to them – though more generally what is supposed to be involved in the relationship of representation is some sort of systematic, causally governed *co-variation* between properties of the images and properties of the 'external' objects.

Now, inasmuch as I have rejected indirect realism, I cannot, of course, wish to support the 'representative theory of perception', as construed in the foregoing traditional terms. However, what I *do* wish to retain from that traditional view is the notion that perceptual processes typically involve relationships of systematic co-variation between properties of perceived objects and certain features of perceptual experience – the latter features being precisely what I have called the *qualitative* ones. So my departure from traditional versions of the 'representative' theory turns mainly on my espousal of an 'adverbialist' rather than an 'act–object' approach to perceptual qualia. As I intimated in the previous section, I even want to retain some aspects of the talk about representation by way of *resemblance*, though now construed in terms of a notion of 'structural isomorphism'.

As an example of representation by way of structural isomorphism, consider the way in which a contour map represents variations in the height of a piece of terrain by the pattern of contour lines drawn on the map. For instance, the presence of lines drawn *closer together* on a portion of the map represents *greater steepness* in the corresponding portion of terrain. This kind of representation of information is sometimes called 'analogue' representation (often in contrast to 'digital' representation): compare the way in which a traditional clock dial represents the passage of time with the way in which this is represented by a digital clock. Times which differ by a small amount are represented on the clock dial by positions which differ by a correspondingly small amount in distance from one another, whereas in a digital clock a small change in time may correspond to either a small or a large change in its digital representation. (Thus although the change in time from 11.59 to 12.00 is equal in value with the change from 12.00 to 12.01, the digital representation of the former change involves a change of four digits whereas that of the latter change involves a change of only one.)

My belief, then, is that a certain amount of 'analogue representation' is involved in human sense-perception, with the qualitative character of perceptual experiences exhibiting patterns of organisation structurally isomorphic to, and co-varying systematically with certain properties and relations of the environmental objects causally implicated in the genesis of those experiences – especially, of course, their geometrical properties of shape and size, and their spatial relationships to one another and to the subject. A simple example may help to give one a sense of what is involved in this proposal, and why it is plausible.

Consider the case in which a normally sighted subject looks at a circular dinner plate held face-on in front of him, and then gradually tips the plate away from himself until he sees it edge-on. This procedure induces a familiar sequence of changes in the qualitative content or character of the subject's visual experience, a sequence we may attempt to capture in everyday language by saying that as the plate is tipped progressively more and more away from the subject it 'looks' more and more acutely elliptical until eventually it presents only a thin, almost linear appearance. What this description of the process brings to light is (a) the existence of a systematic co-variation between certain features of the qualitative character of the subject's visual experience and the orientation of the circular plate relative to the subject, and (b) an element of 'analogue' representation in the relationship between the relevant qualitative features of the visual experience at any given moment and the corresponding shape and orientation of the plate at that moment. That a mode of 'analogue' representation is involved is demonstrated by the fact that small changes in the shape and/or orientation of the plate induce correspondingly small changes in the relevant qualitative features of experience (compare the case of the contour map or the clock dial). In my view, we can go even further and say that *geometrical* modes of description are applicable 'cross-categorially' *both* to qualitative features of visual experience *and* to physical objects in the subject's environment, and indeed that the kind of analogue representation involved here is governed by principles of projective geometry. (For instance, I think that the use of the adjective 'elliptical' in our description of the 'appearance' of the plate reflects the *literal* applicability of just such a geometrical expression to a qualitative feature of visual experience.) This is, admittedly, quite an ambitious and contentious claim – but if it can be sustained, as I believe it can, the upshot will be that Locke was not really so far off the mark in claiming there to be *resemblances* between our ideas of primary qualities and those qualities as they are in the objects.

It may be noticed that the foregoing discussion has rather left to one side the issue of the 'representational' or 'intentional' contents of perceptual experiences. Precisely how these fit into the picture is a complicated business which cannot be gone into in any detail here. The most I can say now is that, in my view, we learn so to interpret our perceptual experiences as to confer upon them specific representational contents, by learning through experience what various sorts of environmental objects 'look like' (or, more generally, how they 'appear') under varying conditions. That is to say, we learn to recognise certain features of the qualitative character of experience as 'signs' (as Locke might say) of certain properties of 'external' objects, and thence invest our experiences with the character of 'presenting' to us objects with precisely those properties. (Of course, this is not normally a conscious process.) Opponents of the Lockean approach are apt to object to this sort of account that it is impossible to take x as a 'sign' of y unless we have independent access to both x and y (for instance, to both dark clouds and rain), and they point out that the Lockean approach precisely denies us independent access to the properties of 'external' objects. I shall return to this area of debate later, but here let me say that I both dispute the foregoing principle concerning signs and believe, in any case, that the objection just mooted is merely a variant of the 'veil of perception' objection to Locke, which I consider to be utterly discredited.

Chapter 4

Substance

A brief history of the notion of substance

The concept of substance is absolutely central to seventeenth–century metaphysics, and is adopted in one form or another by philosophers of widely differing views – both by so-called 'rationalists' like Descartes, Spinoza and Leibniz and by so–called 'empiricists' like Locke and Berkeley. But all of the philosophers just mentioned nonetheless disagree profoundly as to the nature of substance and as to what substances there are in the world. This may make one wonder whether in talking of 'substance' they are really in any sense talking a common language or are just at cross-purposes. In order to get clearer about this issue, we need to delve into the history of the notion of substance, which is traceable at least back to Aristotle, in whose metaphysical writings it plays a fundamental role. And although all of the seventeenth-century philosophers mentioned above (with the partial exception of Leibniz) repudiated much of Aristotle's philosophy – sometimes quite vehemently

– none of them could conceal a very considerable debt to his terminology and influence.

Some of the divergences we find between different seventeenth-century philosophers' conceptions of substance are traceable to different emphases they place on various features of the original Aristotelian doctrine of substance. In one of his important early works, the *Categories*, Aristotle introduces the notion of a 'primary' substance, by which he means, roughly speaking, a concrete, individual, persisting thing – such as a tree, a rock, a house or a man. (It is important, then, to see that this use of the term 'substance' is considerably removed from its most common present-day use, to denote a *kind of stuff*, such as water or potassium chloride – though we shall see some connections emerge in due course.) Aristotle calls such things 'primary' substances in order to distinguish them from what he calls 'secondary' substances, by which he understands the general *kinds* (or *species* or *genera*) to which those things belong. Thus the kind man is the 'secondary' substance to which the individual man Socrates belongs, and Socrates himself is a 'primary' substance.

The *Categories*, as its title suggests, is a work devoted to listing and characterising the various different types of constituents of reality, primary substances being for Aristotle the most basic constituents. Other constituents include such items as *qualities* and *places*, which substances respectively 'have' and 'occupy'. Aristotle implies that the existence of items in these other categories somehow *depends on* the existence of substances, but not vice versa – the dependency is one-sided or asymmetrical. Thus qualities like whiteness and circularity only exist because there are individual substances that are white or circular – the qualities cannot exist, as it were, free–floating and unattached. This ontological asymmetry is reflected in the grammatical fact that qualities are *predicated* of substances, but primary substances themselves are not predicated of anything else.

Another distinctive feature of the primary substances is their capacity to persist identically through qualitative change: a substance can change from being white to being red, or from being circular to being square, while yet remaining the same individual substance (think of a white rubber ball that is dyed red and squashed out of shape). Again, substances exhibit a special kind of *unity* or *cohesion*, giving them a kind of integrity or wholeness which is lacked by items like a pile of rocks or a herd of sheep. Even if a substance has parts (as a finger is part of a man), it is not a mere aggregate or collection of those parts: the whole is somehow greater than the sum of the parts – indeed, the parts are only really defined in terms of their relation to the whole (as a man's heart is the organ which serves to circulate blood in his body).

In a later and still more important work, the *Metaphysics*, Aristotle further elaborates (some say he *changes*) his doctrines concerning substance, by introducing the distinction between *matter* and *form*. Loosely, matter is what a thing is made of and form is the way in which that matter is organised. For the most part, Aristotle seems to espouse a 'relative' conception of matter, whereby different sorts of things have different sorts of matter appropriate to their kind or species. Thus a house is made of bricks and mortar, so that these are its 'matter', and a brick is made of clay and straw, so that these are *its* 'matter', which differs from the 'matter' of the house. Again, the 'matter' of a human being will be flesh and bones. But *form* as well as matter is required to make a single, unified thing: a heap of bricks and mortar is not yet a house. A question which inevitably arises here is this: is it the *form*, or the *matter*, or the whole unified thing that is ontologically most fundamental? If either form or matter is more fundamental than the unified thing, then the latter, although called by Aristotle a 'primary' substance in the *Categories*, will not after all be a fundamental constituent of reality, and hence not really be deserving of the title (primary) substance. Scholars are still divided over the question of Aristotle's final view on this issue, if indeed he had a settled opinion.

A further important ingredient in Aristotle's later writings on substance is his notion of *essence*. He distinguishes between the 'accidental' and the 'essential' properties or qualities of things like men, rocks and trees. Although a primary substance (as I shall continue to call it) can persist through *some* qualitative changes, it cannot persist through all: some changes are 'substantial' changes, because they involve the ceasing-to-be or coming-to-be of an individual substance. Thus a house can survive a change of colour, when it is freshly painted: but it cannot survive dismemberment into a pile of bricks, because its possession of a certain shape is integral to its *form*, and is implied by its being a thing of a certain kind or species (the kind house). A property which a substance cannot lose without thereby ceasing to exist is an *essential* property of that substance – and the sum total of a thing's essential properties constitutes its 'essence' or 'nature'. Clearly, there are intimate connections between the notions of *essence*, *form* and *species* (or kind).

I mentioned earlier that Aristotle mostly (some would say *only*) conceived of matter in 'relative' terms. When a primary substance ceases to be, it is (typically) reduced to its matter – as when a house is reduced to a pile of bricks and mortar. But a brick, too, is a primary substance which can in turn be reduced to *its* matter – and so on and on until, *perhaps*, we reach some sort of ultimate or 'prime' matter which is the basic 'stuff' out of which *everything* in the world is ultimately formed. (There is no *logical* necessity for the hierarchy of matter and form to 'bottom out' in this unitary way – it might not bottom out at all, or might do so in a number of *distinct kinds* of 'ultimate' matter. In many of his writings, Aristotle accepts the traditional doctrine of the four basic 'elements' – earth, water, air and fire – which supposedly compose all things in different proportions, allegedly explaining their different densities and their different chemical properties.) The doctrine of 'prime matter', though not prominent in Aristotle's own writings, was nevertheless to receive strong advocacy in latter times, and may well have influenced Locke's views on substance.

In the mediaeval scholastic period, Aristotelian metaphysics and science were widely accepted, although in considerably modified forms. Seventeenth-century philosophers supporting the new mechanical science of Galileo and Newton completely rejected Aristotelian *science*, but not Aristotle's basic metaphysical vocabulary. The objection to Aristotelian – or, more properly, scholastic – views of the proper explanation of natural phenomena was that they rendered such explanations vacuous and useless. The scholastic approach (though this is mildly to caricature it) was to suppose that the explanation of why a thing behaves as it does – why a stone falls or why (to use Molière's facetious example) opium sends one to sleep – is to be found in an account of the thing's 'essence', or 'nature', or 'substantial form'.

But this only seems to tell us that a thing behaves in the way it does because it is a thing of a kind such that it behaves in that way – that opium sends us to sleep because it is the kind of stuff that makes us sleepy (it has a 'dormitive virtue'). This is neither very enlightening nor very useful in enabling us to predict the behaviour of things not already familiar to us. The great strength of the 'mechanical philosophy' was that it offered the prospect of substantive explanation and useful prediction – prediction which could be stated in precise, quantitative and measurable terms. Instead of being fobbed off with the 'explanation' that a stone falls because it is in its 'nature' to seek the earth, being itself preponderantly made of earth and thus 'heavy', Galileo and Newton can tell us precise mathematical laws relating a stone's velocity to the distance it has fallen in a given time and to the force of gravity to which it is subjected – laws which can also be used to calculate the trajectories of projectiles (something of great value to the developing technology of artillery) and even to predict the motions of the moon and planets.

But the abandonment of Aristotelian science did not bring in its train the wholesale abandonment of Aristotelian metaphysics, even though the concept of substance was to suffer some fragmentation at the hands of seventeenth-century philosophers. Different philosophers placed emphasis on different strands in the Aristotelian doctrine of substance: Leibniz, for instance, emphasising (in his theory of monads) the theme of the *unity* of an individual substance; Spinoza emphasising the theme of the *ontological independence* of substance; and Locke (as we shall see) emphasising the role of substance in its relation to *qualities*.

A further source of division between the major seventeenth–century philosophers was their different attitudes towards the doctrine of *atomism* (traceable to another ancient Greek philosopher, Democritus, but not accepted by Aristotle). In general, the English empiricist philosophers and scientists – Hobbes, Locke, Newton and Boyle, for instance – were sympathetic to atomism, while the continental philosophers, especially Descartes, were hostile. (Like almost all sweeping generalisations, this is only approximately true: Pierre Gassendi (1592-1655), for example, was an important French empiricist who believed in atomism.) For the atomists, each indivisible material atom is an individual substance in its own right, whereas according to Descartes talk of 'atoms and the void' is incoherent: the whole of space is a *plenum* (literally, 'full', with no 'empty' space anywhere), so that the extended material universe as a whole is a single, undivided substance.

So much for matter: but what of *mind*? Aristotle had regarded the human mind or soul as being nothing but the 'form' of the human body, rather than as a separable thing in its own right (though some passages of *De anima* in which he talks of the thinking or rational part of the human soul suggest a different view). Plato, as we saw in Chapter 2 (pp. 15–17), had a very different conception of the soul, and one more congenial to Christian doctrine (in some ways). The Cartesian conception of the soul is more akin to Plato's than to Aristotle's, and indeed Descartes treats it as an individual substance capable of existence separate from the body. Locke likewise seems to adopt this view, though perhaps with some qualms (as we shall see). Thus both Descartes and Locke are *dualists* (more accurately, 'substance dualists') on the question of the relation between soul and body, even though they differ over the nature of body itself on account of their different evaluations of atomism.

Enough has now been said by way of scene-setting, and we can proceed to examine in detail Locke's own views concerning substance – recalling that the 'idea' of substance is one of those ideas whose alleged source in sense-experience he has undertaken to explain in consequence of his repudiation of the doctrine of innate ideas.

Locke on individual substances and substance in general

Locke's extensive discussion of the topic of substance in the *Essay* is highly complex and in places apparently inconsistent – though I think it is possible in the end to unravel a more-or-less coherent account from what he says. We may begin by noting that Locke for the most part goes along with the Aristotelian tradition of calling concrete, individual persisting things – like trees, rocks and men – *particular substances*, acknowledging too that these are classifiable into various different *sorts* or *species*. In contrast with this notion of *substance*, he also uses another Aristotelian (or, more properly, scholastic) term, *mode*, to speak of the various particular *qualities* or *properties* that particular substances possess – properties of shape, colour, weight and the like. (Locke classifies modes as being either 'simple' or 'mixed' (2.12.5); roughly speaking, what distinguishes 'mixed modes' for Locke is their partially mind–dependent status (2.22.2), his examples being such characteristics as beauty and hypocrisy.)

However, Locke is at the same time somewhat ambivalent about the substantial status of ordinary, macroscopic objects like trees, animals and rocks, because they do not, in his view, belong amongst what we might call the fundamental constituents of reality (as Alston & Bennett (1988) have pointed out). Indeed, it would appear that for Locke there are just *three* sorts of substance in this ultimate sense: individual material atoms, individual 'finite spirits' (including human souls), and God (an 'infinite' spirit). He even remarks that 'all other things [are] but Modes or Relations ultimately terminated in Substances [of these three sorts]' (2.27.2). According to this stricter account, the individual things such as trees and animals which we (and Locke himself, most of the time) are apt to speak of as 'substances' more accurately have the status of 'modes' (albeit highly complex ones) attributable to genuine or ultimate substances of the three sorts just mentioned. (Thus in the case of trees, say, the ultimate substances in question will obviously be material atoms.) That such macroscopic physical objects should have the ontological status of modes was nothing peculiar to Locke's philosophy, since Spinoza, and on some accounts Descartes too, held a similar view for reasons of their own (though in their case such objects were modes not of material atoms, of course, but rather of the single substance which, in their view, constituted the extended physical universe as a whole).

Since Locke mostly ignores this 'stricter' doctrine regarding substance, so shall we in the remainder of this section. His main concern with the notion of substance, as I mentioned in the previous section, is in its connection with the notion of the *qualities* of a thing: in particular, he is clearly much impressed by the thought that the qualities of a concrete, persisting thing are subject to a condition of ontological dependency upon something belonging to a quite different category – they cannot exist free-floating and unattached, as it were, but need to be 'anchored' in something more self-subsistent in its nature. This thought is clearly uppermost when he declares, at one point, that 'not imagining how ... simple *Ideas* can subsist by them-selves, we accustom our selves to suppose some *Substratum*, wherein they do subsist' (2.23.1). I should, incidentally, point out at once that in order to interpret correctly this passage and many others like it, we need to recall the fact mentioned above (p. 19) that Locke, by his own confession, often carelessly uses the term 'idea' when he really intends to talk about the *quality* (in an 'external' object) which gives rise to a particular idea in us. Thus when he says, in these passages, that we conceive of *ideas* as needing something which supports them or in which they subsist or 'inhere', he is not pointing out (though he would in fact agree with this also) that *mental states* must be states of a sub-stance of some kind (probably of a 'spirit' or 'soul'), but rather that the *qualities* of physical objects which cause these ideas in us require sup-port by some 'external', *material* 'substratum'.

On the face of it, Locke's talk about 'substratum', or what he also calls 'pure substance in general' (2.23.2), seems to involve a conflation of two separate notions: one is the notion of there being a relation of ontological dependency between qualities and the indi-vidual substances or 'things' of which they are qualities, and the other is the somewhat dubious notion of 'prime matter', which we encoun-tered in the previous section. It is not obvious that these two notions *need* to be connected, but Locke does seem in many places to be sug-gesting that the *reason* why individual substances are entities capable of sustaining this sort of dependency-relation to qualities is that such substances have as an 'underlying' ingredient something like prime matter, which somehow serves to 'anchor' the qualities of an individ-ual substance and 'hold them together' as qualities of a single thing – as though the roundness and whiteness of a particular rubber ball have to 'stick to' (or, as Locke says, 'inhere in') some basic underlying stuff in order to stay together as qualities of the same ball. (Of course, we *do* suppose that a rubber ball is made of 'stuff' – namely, rubber – but, as we shall see, there is some pressure to regard the ultimate 'sub-stratum' as more basic than any specific *kind* of stuff, such as rubber or gold.)

The trouble (or *one* trouble) with this notion of a basic underly-ing 'stuff' is, as Locke himself acknowledges, that we have, and appar-ently *can* have, no 'positive' idea of it, but at most a 'relative' idea of it as 'something we know not what' which somehow 'supports' the qualities of individual substances (2.23.2). This would be a particular embarrassment for Locke as an empiricist committed to explaining how all our ideas arise from perceptual experience.

The reason, it seems, why we *can* have no 'positive' idea of the basic underlying stuff or substratum is twofold. First, all our positive ideas are of *qualities*, for these are what we can perceive by means of our senses (by way of ideas): but qualities are what the 'stuff' supposedly *supports*, rather than the stuff itself. Second, and even more mysteriously, it seems as though the stuff or substratum itself *cannot have qualities of its own*, for its ontological role is to support the qualities *of an individual substance or 'thing'*, and the latter is not to be identified with the substratum providing such 'support'. In itself, it seems, the substratum must be utterly featureless – for *if* it had qualities of its own, then these would, by the same train of reasoning, require some *yet more basic* 'stuff' to 'support' *them*. But now we appear to be embroiled in absurdity: for if the basic stuff or substratum is utterly *featureless*, what is it about it that enables it to perform its supposed role of 'supporting' qualities – how is an utterly featureless 'something' different from *nothing at all*?

Clearly, there is something wrong with this whole picture; but perhaps we have been too hasty in ascribing this sort of view to Locke himself, even though many commentators do. Recalling Aristotle's 'relative' notion of matter, explained in the previous section, might we not suggest that something more like this is in Locke's mind when he talks of 'substratum'? And recalling, too, Locke's sympathy for atomism, might we not suppose that what he understands by the 'substratum' of a macroscopic object like a tree is the complex, organised assembly of material atoms that are its ultimate substantial constituents – what he elsewhere calls the 'real essence' of such an object (compare Ayers 1991, II, pp. 31ff; and, for an opposing view, see Bennett 1987)? After all, in view of Locke's allegiance to the 'mechanical philosophy', we know that he is sympathetic to the notion that all of the observable, macroscopic qualities of a large-scale object – its weight, density, colour, shape, and so forth – are in principle explicable in terms of the primary qualities and organisation of its microstructural constituents. It is the latter that *genuinely* explain, if anything does, why the large-scale object has these properties, and why they 'hang together' as they do. And, indeed, there are passages which suggest precisely this 'sensible' reading of Locke's text, for instance, where he says:

> we come to have the *Ideas of particular sorts of Substances*, by collecting such Combinations of simple *Ideas*, as are by Experience . . . taken notice of to exist together, and are therefore supposed to flow from the particular internal Constitution, or unknown Essence of that Substance (2.23.3).

For it is clear in other passages that by 'internal constitution' and 'unknown [real] essence' Locke means the microstructural atomic organisation of a macroscopic object. But this is a far cry from some supposedly featureless basic 'stuff' or 'prime matter'. For the atoms *have* qualities (albeit only primary ones) and are related to one another in quite specific ways. Our ignorance of these atomic constitutions of things is (or *was*, in Locke's day, since we now know a good deal about them) an entirely *contingent* ignorance, stemming from inadequate technology, not a *necessary* ignorance stemming from the supposed fact that there is *nothing to know* about 'substratum'.

Unfortunately, this sensible and sanitised interpretation of Locke's position is compromised by certain passages, and indeed to some extent by the very logic of the substance/mode distinction that Locke has adopted from his scholastic predecessors, at least in the form in which he seems to understand it. The point is that substratum, for Locke, seems to have a *metaphysical* role to play above and beyond any merely *scientific* explanatory role which could be offered by the doctrine of atomism. For, precisely because individual material atoms *themselves* have a multiplicity of qualities (even if we cannot detect them, lacking the technology to do so), the metaphysical question of what 'supports' these qualities and makes them 'stick together' as qualities of a single atom can still be asked, if it is ever proper to ask such a question at all. That Locke himself felt the force of this point is indicated by the following remark of his:

> If anyone should be asked, what is the subject wherein Colour or Weight inheres, he would have nothing to say, but the solid

extended parts: And if he were demanded, what is it, that that
Solidity and Extension inhere in, [he would . . . have to reply]
something, he knew not what. (2.23.2)

The only way, it seems, to avoid the conclusion of this line of reasoning is to reject altogether the 'inherence' model of the relation between
substance and quality (what has sometimes been derisively called the
'pin-cushion' model). Locke, I suspect, saw no clear way of avoiding
this model – though I shall propose one myself in this chapter (pp.
87–91). Had he been able to see one, I think that the broad outlines
of his doctrine concerning substance – including a 'sanitised' notion of
'substratum' in terms of internal, microstructural constitution – could
have been represented as both tenable and plausible.

Can it be said, however, that Locke comes at all close to success
on his own terms in providing an 'empiricist' account of our idea(s)
of substance, without needing to fall back on any innate notions?
I think not, because he seems to be convinced that only the *qualities*
of physical objects are perceptible to us by way of ideas, and the idea
of substance is not the idea of any quality or combination of qualities.
Descartes, who appears to have had a similar view of our powers
of perception, has a way out of this problem, urging that 'we can . . .
easily come to know a substance by one of its attributes, in virtue of
the common notion that nothingness possesses no attributes, that is to
say, no properties or qualities' (*Principles of Philosophy*, I, 52). This
'common notion' is, of course, an innate idea (or rather principle)
according to Descartes, requiring no source in sense-experience. But
Locke has excluded any such appeal to innate ideas as unwarranted
and superfluous.

Locke's problem is not, I think, merely an artefact of the mis-
conceived 'inherence' model of the substance/quality relation, however. It is not enough, either, simply to urge that we do, after all,
perceive physical *objects* as well as their *qualities*. What is required is
some account of the origin and basis of the categorial framework
which we bring to bear in interpreting our sense-experience: and it
may possibly be that Kant was right in supposing that this is not so
much something that we do or could discover *in* experience and
can justify on that basis, as something that we ourselves contribute to

our understanding of the natural world that is revealed to us by experience. This need not be to regard that categorial framework as being in any sense subjective or arbitrary – as not reflecting real and mind–independent objective distinctions in nature – since, on a naturalistic account of the development of the human mind one would expect the cast of our mind to have been shaped to accommodate structures really existing in the world of which it is a part, and which it has evolved to know.

Locke's distinction between 'real' and 'nominal' essences

Locke's discussion of essence in the *Essay* is considerably complicated by the fact that he is at once both attempting to explain and criticise what he takes to have been the development of this notion in the scholastic philosophy deriving from Aristotle, and recommending certain views of his own. He claims that in the 'proper original signification' of the word 'essence' it denotes 'the very being of any thing, whereby it is, what it is' (3.3.15) (a definition which is, one has to admit, far from perspicuous). Although he then goes on to suggest that the Scholastics misappropriated the word 'essence' to talk about 'genus and species', I think what he means is that the Scholastics adopted a *mistaken theory* concerning the nature of essence (in its 'proper' sense) which led them to associate distinctions of essence with distinctions of species and genus. The theory in question was the theory of *substantial forms*, of which Locke speaks extremely slightingly. This is the theory which, according to Locke, sees '*Essences*, as a certain number of Forms or Moulds, wherein all natural Things, that exist, are cast, and do equally partake [of]' (3.3.17). As Locke sees it, this theory mistakenly attempted to appeal to 'forms' to explain *both* 'the very being of any thing, whereby it is, what it is' *and* at the same time our classification of things into different kinds (species and genera). A particular thing, on this view, 'is what it is' by virtue of being cast in a certain 'form', and is classifiable alongside other things as being of the same *kind* by virtue of the fact that all of these things are cast in the *same* 'form'. Hence, Locke suggests, under the influence of this mistaken theory, we have come to think of a thing's essence, or of its 'essential properties', as being those of its features that are implied by its membership of a given *sort* or *kind*.

Locke seems resigned to the fact – as he sees it – that the notion of essence has become distorted in this way, and is prepared to go along with the new usage, though not, of course, with the theory which he regards as being responsible for it. For he himself has a quite different theory of how and why things are classified into kinds in the ways they are, urging that 'Things are ranked under Names into sorts or *Species*, only as they agree to certain abstract *Ideas*, to which we have annexed those Names' (3.3.15). (We shall explore Locke's theory of abstract ideas more fully in Chapter 7.) And, in Locke's view, the considerations which lead us to form certain abstract ideas to which we 'annex' the names of species and genera have very little if anything to do with 'the very being of any thing, whereby it is, what it is' – that is, with what he calls '*real* essence' – at least in the case of substances. (In the case of modes he is happy to concede that real and nominal essence coincide, but we shall not pursue this point any further here.) In the case of a substance, its real essence is its 'unknown constitution' upon which its discoverable qualities 'depend' – that is, its micro-structural organisation understood in accordance with the atomic, mechanical theory of matter favoured by Locke and leading English scientists of his day.

We can sum up the situation by saying that, according to Locke, we now have *two* notions of essence, one *explanatory* and the other *classificatory*, the first 'proper' and 'original' and the second the product of a mistaken theory but now an ineradicable part of our language. In Locke's view, the substantial forms of the Scholastics were supposed by them to play *both* of these roles, whereas according to Locke, at least in the case of substances, they are played by two quite different sorts of thing – internal microstructural constitutions on the one hand ('real' essences), and abstract general ideas on the other ('nominal' essences). The diagram on the following page depicts this state of affairs, as Locke seems to see it.

We now need to examine both what Locke thought to be wrong in the scholastic theory of essence and what he considers to be the merits of his own opposing view. It is clear, first of all, that he does not consider that substantial forms provide any genuine *explanation* at

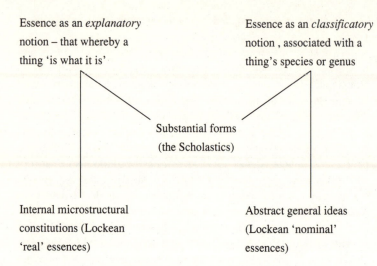

Essence as an *explanatory* notion – that whereby a thing 'is what it is'

Essence as an *classificatory* notion , associated with a thing's species or genus

Substantial forms
(the Scholastics)

Internal microstructural constitutions (Lockean 'real' essences)

Abstract general ideas (Lockean 'nominal' essences)

all for the nature of things: this is part and parcel of the rejection by Locke and his mechanistically minded contemporaries of the whole framework of Aristotelian science, as modified by the Scholastics (see again the first section of this chapter). But he also considers that the doctrine of substantial forms fails even as an account of our *classificatory* practices, remarking that

> the *supposition of Essences, that cannot be known*; and the making them nevertheless to be that, which distinguishes the Species of Things, *is so wholly useless* . . . [as] to make us lay it by. (3.3.17)

To this may be added his observation that 'the frequent Productions of Monsters, in all the Species of Animals . . . [cannot] consist with this *Hypothesis*' (3.3.17). So the thought is that the supposed 'forms' or 'moulds' favoured by the Scholastics are entirely the product of metaphysical speculation without any empirical basis, whence they cannot be what *actually* serve to guide us in classifying particulars into different sorts or species – but that, furthermore, to the extent that the metaphor (for that is what it is) of a 'mould' has any implications at all for the generation of sorts or species, it would seem to imply that all particulars cast in the same 'mould' ought to be exactly alike, contrary to the wide variations which we actually recognise amongst members of what we regard as the same animal species.

The second of these points is not perhaps all that compelling (after all, to pursue the 'mould' metaphor, some castings can be defective, with parts missing or cracked). As to the first and apparently stronger point – that we cannot classify particulars by reference to a supposed feature of them which is unknown to us – Locke is adamant that this is why we also cannot classify substances according to what he calls their 'real' essences (their microstructural constitutions), for these are (or were in his day) unknown to us, and even if they did become known could not be expected (Locke thinks) to have a bearing upon our linguistic practices, 'since Languages, in all Countries, have been established long before Sciences' (3.6.25).

Without wishing to provide succour for the scholastic account of essence (at least as relayed to us via Locke), I think it is clear that this apparently persuasive point of Locke's is again open to dispute: for it is arguable (and indeed *has* been argued by modern philosophers like Hilary Putnam (1975)) that even accepting Locke's own view of the 'real' essences of substances and the difficulty of our coming to know them, it is plausible to contend that our classificatory practices both *aim* at and often *succeed* in grouping substances by reference to their 'real' essences, as opposed to their supposed 'nominal' essences. (Locke recognises that we sometimes *aim* to do this – as John Mackie (1976, pp. 93ff.) has pointed out – but condemns the attempt as mistaken and doomed to failure (3.10.17-3.10.19).)

Consider, for instance, one of Locke's own favourite examples of a kind-term denoting a species of substance – 'gold'. The particulars falling under this general term will be various individual pieces or quantities of metal, which we classify together as being things of the same kind. Now, according to Locke, the 'nominal' essence of gold which, he contends, forms the basis of our classification of particulars under the term 'gold', is an 'abstract general idea' comprising the ideas of various *observable qualities* – qualities like yellow colour and shiny appearance, hardness, heaviness, malleability and ductility (to which we may perhaps add various empirically detectable chemical and physical properties, such as solubility in *aqua regia* and a readiness to conduct heat). But notice that most and perhaps all of these observable qualities and properties may be possessed by substances that are *not* gold, while on the other hand things that really *are* gold may *lack* many of these qualities (liquid gold, for instance, is neither hard, nor malleable, nor ductile). We are all familiar with the term 'fool's gold', which in fact refers to iron pyrites, a substance which deceives the unwary prospector precisely because it has all the outward *appearance* of gold but is not 'really' gold. But this entire way of talking, which ordinary language endorses, suggests that we are ready to distinguish between a 'real' instance of some natural, substantial kind and a merely 'apparent' instance of it which shares the same outward, observable appearance. And this seems to conflict with Locke's insistence that the classification of kinds of substance must proceed by reference to readily observable characteristics alone.

What then *does* make something 'really' gold? Today we would say that it is internal atomic constitution (none other than Lockean 'real essence') that does this: real gold is composed of atoms containing 79 protons in their nuclei. But this was unknown to anyone in Locke's day, and is only known to those with a scientific education today – and even many of the latter would be unable to *tell* whether or not a piece of metal contained such atoms. So how can such a consideration have any bearing on how, as members of a linguistic community, we actually *use* the word 'gold' in ordinary speech? Must Locke not be right in saying that it can have *no* bearing? Not necessarily. For Locke is ignoring what Putnam (1975) has called the 'division of linguistic labour'. Non-experts typically defer to the opinion of experts with regard to the reference of natural kind-terms. As a non–expert I may indeed base my initial decision to call a piece of metal 'gold' upon its outward observable appearance (what Putnam would call my 'stereotype' of gold): but I am always prepared to withdraw my description should an expert in chemical analysis tell me that the metal does not in fact have the right chemical composition. In a sense, this principle even operates retrospectively, to sanction or condemn as mistaken attempted references to gold made even before current methods of chemical analysis were available. This permits us to say that our forebears in Locke's time were indeed talking about the same kind of substance as we do today in using the word 'gold' – the 'meaning' of the word has not simply changed in consequence of advances in scientific knowledge. Against Locke, then, we could urge that even ordinary speakers ignorant of science, whether in Locke's time or today, quite properly *intend* to classify substances by reference to their supposed 'real' essences, and in many cases their actual practice of classification can be revealed as satisfying those intentions or not in the light of knowledge available to experts to whom those speakers are prepared to defer.

This is not the place to pursue this debate any further, though certainly there is more to be said on Locke's side, perhaps when suitable adjustments are made to his position. Putnam's account of the semantics of natural kind-terms is certainly not problem-free. But at least it is a testimony to the depth of Locke's philosophical insight that this issue is still debated in the terms in which he originally framed the problem.

The criticisms of Berkeley and Hume

It is hardly surprising that later empiricist-minded philosophers should have pounced upon those awkward passages in which Locke speaks of 'pure substance in general' or 'substratum' as being 'something we know not what' which mysteriously 'supports' the observable qualities of things, and in which those qualities 'inhere'. Both Berkeley and Hume dismiss the metaphors of support and inherence with derision, and neither can tolerate the suggestion of a thing's being any more than the collection of its perceptible qualities. Indeed, they go further by collapsing Locke's distinction between ideas and qualities altogether: what we call 'things' – trees, apples, rocks and so on – are, Berkeley insists, simply collections of ideas and thus have no existence independent of the mind.

Berkeley's attack on matter partly rests, as we saw in the preceding chapter, upon his criticism of Locke's distinction between primary and secondary qualities. Berkeley's strategy is first to argue that qualities like shape and size are inseparable from qualities like colour, so that it is unintelligible to suppose there to be things which possess the former but not the latter. Then he trades upon a general presumption, traces of which we find in Locke's own writings, that the so-called secondary qualities like colour and warmth exist 'only in the mind', in the form of our *ideas* or *sensations* of colour and warmth, in order to conclude that the so-called primary qualities, being inseparable from colour and warmth and the like, must similarly exist 'only in the mind', by way of *ideas*.

Though Berkeley's reasoning can certainly be questioned at many points, it is by no means the tissue of sophistry that many critics claim it to be. I have already conceded, in the previous chapter, the force of Berkeley's charge that the supposedly 'objective' world of classical physics, populated by material particles possessing only the primary qualities, is doubtfully intelligible. But we should distinguish this claim both from the stronger Berkeleian claim that the notion of *any* sort of mind–independent 'external' world is unintelligible and also from his specific objections to the doctrine of the material 'substratum'. One might agree with his rejection of 'substratum' while yet defending the 'world of physics', and one might reject the world of physics while yet defending the existence of a mind–independent 'external' world (one invested with the colours and smells apparently disclosed by human experience).

A curious feature of Berkeley's position, by comparison with Hume's, is that he is not opposed to the notion of substance *as such*. He allows, as Locke and Descartes do, that 'finite spirits' (including human souls) are substances, and indeed that *ideas* depend for their existence upon these mental substances – the dependency being formulated in terms of his famous *esse est percipi* principle (the principle that, for an idea, 'to be is to be perceived'). One might have supposed that this would have led Berkeley to regard ideas as *modes* of mental substances (as on the 'adverbialist' approach discussed at pp. 42–7 above), but in fact he opts in his mature works for an act–object analysis of our relation to our ideas, whereby in 'perceiving' them we stand in a genuine relation to them – the awkwardness of this being that, by Berkeley's own account, they do not exist independently of this relation. A question which naturally arises, therefore, is why Berkeley did not consider that his objections to Locke's conception of *material* substance should not apply equally to his own (and Locke's) conception of *mental* substance or 'spirit'. If the 'inherence' model is untenable for the former, then so it surely is also for the latter; and, conversely, if an acceptable alternative model is available in the case of mental substance, why should it not be equally applicable in the case of material substance? Answering these questions on Berkeley's behalf would take us too far afield, though a hint in that direction is that Berkeley regarded the mind as *active* in a way which he thought contrasted with the 'passivity' both of ideas and of Lockean matter. (He also seems to have believed that we have access to a special kind of knowledge of ourselves through our very exercise of agency, knowledge which is not had by way of *idea* – for Berkeley denies that we have *any* 'idea' of spirit, in line with his 'likeness principle' that 'an idea can be like nothing but an idea'.)

Hume, however, has no time for Berkeley's half-way house: as well as pouring scorn on Locke's conception of material substance, he dismisses too the notion of mental or spiritual substance, the 'soul' or 'self', considered as something *having* ideas but not reducible to them. This is the sub-text of his famous remark that

> when I enter most intimately into what I call *myself*, I always stumble on some particular perception or other, of heat or cold, light or shade, love or hatred, pain or pleasure. I never can catch *myself* at any time without a perception, and never can observe any thing but the perception. (Hume 1978, p. 252)

We may question, as Berkeley does, any attempt to offer a *perceptual* model of our knowledge of the self, observing that even if such a model fails for the reason Hume gives, some other model (such as Berkeley's own *agency* model) may be available. We may also query Hume's apparent presumption that the only conception of the substance/quality distinction that is on offer is the seriously flawed one provided by the 'inherence' account. To reject this account need not be to reject every possible conception of substance.

To do justice to Hume's objections we should, however, give some consideration to another claim he makes a little earlier in the *Treatise* (ibid., p. 233). There he contends, in effect, that the whole notion of *ontological independence*, and with it the correlative notion of *ontological dependency*, is vacuous – because the former notion applies to *everything* and the latter correspondingly to *nothing*. Since the doctrine of substance from its Aristotelian inception turns crucially on these notions, it can only be salvaged if Hume is mistaken in his claim. But I think it is clear that he *is* mistaken, and indeed that this mistake is at the root of the disastrous failure of his own system of metaphysics and epistemology, a failure he dimly recognised himself at times.

The mistake stems from Hume's unswerving allegiance to the atomistic principle that

> every thing, which is different, is distinguishable, and every thing which is distinguishable is separable ... and may exist separately, and have no need of any thing else to support [its] existence. (ibid., p. 233)

(In calling this principle 'atomistic', I do not mean to imply that it is a component of *material* atomism, of the scientific sort favoured by Locke; Hume's atomism is of a far deeper *metaphysical* variety.) Hume is denying the existence of any *necessary connections* in nature (not just, I should add, the existence of such connections where a *causal* relationship is thought to obtain, but their existence *tout court*). But he is manifestly wrong in denying this. Examples of necessary connections between things abound. For instance, an edge cannot exist without a surface, a hole cannot exist without a surround, and – very arguably – a perception or idea cannot exist without a perceiving subject (though whether we must conceive of the latter as a 'finite spirit', or 'soul', is an altogether different issue). Certainly, on the 'adverbialist' account of ideas explained above (pp. 42–7), there are manifestly necessary connections between ideas and subjects, for by that account 'ideas' just *are* subjects' *ways of sensing*. A strong case could, I think, be made out for saying that the initial error leading to Hume's untenable position was a certain natural preference, fostered by grammatical considerations, for the act–object analysis over the adverbial analysis of sensation. Once 'ideas' (or 'perceptions') are reified as things *perceived* by subjects or 'selves', it is but a short step to Hume's conclusion that selves are really 'nothing but' collections of ideas (or 'bundles of perceptions'), rather than genuine 'substances' in the Aristotelian sense.

To sum up the discussion of this section: Locke's successors wrought great destruction on his philosophy of substance, opening up thereby the high road to idealism – a doctrine far more deeply riddled with absurdity and confusion than anything we find in Locke's position. But to the extent that their criticisms of Locke's account are sound, they focus on aspects of that account which can arguably be jettisoned without abandoning its general thrust and its realist implications. Locke was right to defend the notion of substance: its abandonment was a disaster for the subsequent course of metaphysics, a disaster which has still not properly been overcome today.

The revival of substance in modern ontology

After a rather bleak period, interest in problems relating to the notion of substance has begun to be revived amongst modern philosophers (along with a more general appreciation of the importance of metaphysics). Two particular areas of current focus may be mentioned immediately: issues to do with the *identity and individuation* of objects on the one hand, and issues to do with what Locke called 'real essence' on the other. The first set of issues will receive more attention in the next chapter. The second set has to do with the semantics of 'natural kind-terms', like 'gold' and 'tiger', and was touched upon earlier (at pp. 78–83): I shall not pursue these issues further here, though they will briefly surface again in Chapter 7. My focus in this section will be, rather, on the core notion of substance itself, which I shall attempt to make somewhat clearer than Locke himself managed to.

As so often in philosophy, we do well in the philosophy of substance to return, at least initially, to Aristotle – and in particular to his notion of a 'primary' substance as presented in the *Categories*. Such a substance is, we recall, conceived to be a concrete, individual persisting thing, a bearer of qualities which is capable of surviving changes in at least some of those qualities, not itself predicable of anything else, and constituting a unified whole rather than a mere aggregate of other things. It certainly does appear that many of the large–scale objects that populate our world satisfy this general description – examples being animals, plants, people, houses, cars, planets and stars. The problems begin, however, when we try to add to this picture the further Aristotelian distinction between matter and form, bringing in its train the distinction between essence and accident.

Part of the difficulty lies in the fact that the term 'matter' is ambiguous as between meaning 'what a thing is *composed* of' and meaning '*stuff* of a certain kind'. Of course, in some cases the two meanings can coincide, in the sense that some things simply *are* composed of stuff of a certain kind: for instance, a solid rubber ball is composed of *rubber*. But very often the question of what a thing is composed of will not be answered (directly, at least) by reference to some kind of stuff. A wall is made of bricks, and a watch is made of cogs and springs. Even so, we may be tempted to presume that if we go on asking what the components of the components of a thing are composed of, and so on and on, we shall eventually come to a point at which reference will *have* to be made to a kind of stuff – as when bricks are said to be made of *clay*, or cogs of *steel*. Bricks just *are* portions of clay baked into a certain shape or *form*, and cogs are portions of steel cut into a certain shape or form. So we might be persuaded to suppose that the 'ultimate' constituents of all 'substantial' things are portions of 'informed' (shaped) *stuff* or *matter* of various kinds (including, perhaps, mixtures of different kinds of stuffs).

But now we have to reflect that, according to modern atomic theory, portions of stuff – say, of butter or gold or rubber – are not perfectly undifferentiated throughout their extension, but are in fact composed of yet further 'things' – atoms and molecules – which in turn have various 'components' (protons, neutrons and electrons). According to classical atomism (as opposed to modern quantum theory), atoms were literally *indivisible* portions of matter possessing some immutable shape ('atom' literally meaning 'uncuttable'). But such a picture of the ultimate constituents of physical reality is now believed to be incorrect. The fundamental 'particles' of modern physics (such as electrons and quarks) neither are composed of any kind of 'stuff', nor have determinate 'shapes'. They do, however, have properties or qualities (like rest mass, charge, kinetic energy, and 'spin'), and they do persist through time and change: so they would seem to qualify as 'substances' in the original Aristotelian sense. It appears, thus, that it makes perfect sense to talk of a primary substance which is not *composed* of anything further – neither of smaller 'things', nor of 'stuff' of any sort. If that is correct, then it cannot be necessary for a substance to have 'matter', in either sense of the term mentioned earlier; and consequently, contrary to Aristotle's later doctrine, we need not conceive of a substance as necessarily involving some sort of combination of 'matter' and 'form'. Some substances are *complex*, in the sense of being composed of or constituted by other things or stuff, but there can in principle also be *simple* substances, which are not.

What is crucial, then, to the notion of substance is not the idea that a substance is a combination of matter and form, but rather the notion of substance as a bearer of (possibly changeable) qualities. Locke, we recall, supposed (in some passages of the *Essay*, at least) that the qualities of an individual substance require a 'substratum' for their 'support' – where the notion of 'substratum' is that of some very basic and indefinite kind of 'stuff'. (The interpretation of 'substratum' as 'real essence' is quite another and more respectable strand of Locke's thought.) But it now emerges that, since there can be *matter-less* substances, it must just be a mistake to try to explain the connection between an individual substance and its qualities in terms of a model which has those qualities 'inhere' in an underlying material substratum, or 'matter'. The 'matter' which such a model invokes is something which richly deserves Berkeley's ridicule of it.

So how, then, *should* we explain the connection between an individual substance and its qualities? The very first thing to observe here is that it is highly misleading to regard these qualities as 'things' of a special sort, standing in some genuine *relation* to the substance which 'has' them. To take this view is to opt for the counterpart of an 'act–object' rather than an 'adverbialist' analysis of our talk of 'having ideas' (or sensations). Indeed, the latter is no mere analogy, but just a special case of the more general point about substances and qualities. For ideas or sensations just are, properly speaking, *qualities* of persons or subjects, and subjects are quite rightly to be called 'substances' in the original Aristotelian sense. (To be perfectly accurate, it is *sensings* that are 'adjectival' upon subjects, while particular 'ideas' or sensations are *modes of sensing*, and thus have an 'adverbial' status – hence the name 'adverbialism' for this view of the ontological status of sensations.)

The lesson, then, is not to treat such qualities as the redness and roundness of a rubber ball as 'things' somehow *related* to the ball – provoking the unanswerable, because absurd, questions of how that mysterious relation 'ties' the qualities to the ball and what the ball is like 'in itself', considered 'separately' from its qualities. Rather, those qualities are best conceived as 'ways the ball is' – literally as 'modifications' or 'modes' of the ball. If it is then asked what the ball *is* over and above the sum of its qualities – what, as it were, 'remains' when these are fully taken into account – we should be tempted *neither* to say that *nothing* else remains because the ball just *is* the sum total of its qualities, *nor* to say that something further *does* remain, in the form of an unknowable, featureless 'substratum' or 'inner core'. Rather, we should reject the question altogether as involving, quite literally, a *category mistake*. The ball and its qualities are not members of the same ontological category, to be placed on either side of some queer kind of arithmetical equation, or metaphysical set of scales. The qualities of an individual substance, such as the redness and roundness of a particular ball, are *ontologically dependent* upon that substance: there could not so much as *be* the redness and roundness of a given ball but for the existence of that ball, but the ball can perfectly well continue to exist without continuing to be red and round. It is not as though the redness of the ball could, like the Cheshire Cat's grin, continue to exist by itself while the ball disappeared into thin air – nor could its redness somehow 'migrate' to another ball.

All such absurd ways of talking derive from the mistaken reification – or, more accurately, the mistaken 'hypostatisation' (= substantification) – of qualities as ontologically independent entities in their own right. Whether these absurd ways of talking arise – as Wittgenstein might have said – from our being misled by grammar, or have deeper roots than that, we need to recognise them as indeed being absurd in order to put an end to some of the interminable debates and confusions that have centred around the notion of substance for centuries, serving only to bring that indispensable metaphysical notion into disrepute. There are substances in the world and there are qualities, but we have to accept that they involve fundamentally distinct and mutually irreducible 'modes of being', which are nonetheless only understandable by reference to one another. Such irreducible plurality can only seem mysterious or repugnant to philosophers driven by the sort of quest for simplicity that led to the quagmire of Humean atomism. It is to Locke's great credit as a philosopher that he did not allow his sound common sense to be overriden by the urge for such spurious profundity in metaphysics. That, at bottom, is why he does not abandon the category of substance despite the difficulty he finds in accommodating it within his empiricist framework.

Chapter 5

Identity

Sortal terms and criteria of identity

Many philosophers have observed that there is an important distinction to be drawn between two broad classes of general terms, though the vocabulary they use to mark the distinction varies considerably. Some, like P. T. Geach (1980, p. 63), talk of the distinction between 'adjectival' and 'substantival' general terms; others, like P. F. Strawson (1959, p. 168), speak instead of the distinction between 'characterising' and 'sortal' general terms – the latter expression apparently being a coinage of Locke himself (3.3.15). Taking a general term to be any expression (whether simple or complex) which is univocally applicable to many different individuals, such as 'green', 'round', 'tree' or 'mountain', we may say that the *adjectival* or *characterising* general terms are ones like 'green' and 'round', while the *substantival* or *sortal* general terms are ones like 'tree' and 'mountain'. (Henceforth I shall speak just of 'adjectival' and 'sortal' general terms.)

The difference between the two classes of terms is best captured by using some terminology of Michael Dummett (1981, pp. 73ff.), who remarks that whereas adjectival general terms have associated with their use only a *criterion of application*, sortal terms have associated with them not only a criterion of application but also a *criterion of identity*. The first kind of criterion is a principle determining to *which* individuals the general term in question is correctly applicable, while the second kind of criterion is a principle determining the conditions under which one individual to which the term is applicable is *the same* as another. (As always when talking about identity, one must be cautious in speaking of one individual being identical with 'another' because, of course, each individual can really only be identical with *itself*: the way of speaking in question, though convenient and idiomatic, needs to be understood as properly a shorthand way of talking about an individual *referred to* in one way being identical with an individual – the *same* one! – *referred to* in another way. Provided that this is clearly understood, the idiom is harmless enough.)

Consider, then, the general terms 'green' and 'tree'. Each *applies* to some things and not to others, and the relevant criteria of application should tell us which things these are. Thus a particular tree, a particular leaf on that tree and a particular caterpillar on that leaf are all *green things*. As it happens, they are all *different* green things. But nothing about the meaning of the term 'green' helps to guide us in determining whether or not those things are different. By contrast, in the case of the general term 'tree', we not only have a criterion of application which tells us which things are trees and which are not, we also receive guidance from the meaning of that term regarding the conditions which determine whether one tree is the same as or different from another. Because, and only because, we have such guidance, in the form of a *criterion of identity* for trees, we are able to *count* or *enumerate* trees, and can thereby hope to answer a question like 'How many *trees* are there in that wood?' The task of counting them may be a difficult one, but we know that it is in principle achievable. Matters are otherwise, however, if someone asks us the question 'How many *green things* are there in that wood?' In this case, we simply do not even know how to *begin* counting, because we do not know what *sorts* of things to count. ('Green things' do not collectively constitute a *sort*, precisely because there is no single criterion of identity governing all green things.) For example, suppose we tried to begin by counting green *leaves* in the wood: then, even before we could count the first leaf, we would have to decide whether each green *part* of that leaf was to count as a distinct 'green thing' to be included in the overall enumeration. But how do we count the green parts of a leaf? We can divide a leaf into parts in innumerable different ways – for instance, into squares, or into triangles, and these of various different sizes. Clearly, the 'task' of counting 'all' the green things in a wood is not just impossible *in practice*, but impossible *in principle* – because, in the absence of any appropriate criterion of identity, we simply do not know where to begin, where to stop, and how to avoid counting the same thing twice.

An important thing to appreciate about criteria of identity is that different sortal terms often – though by no means always – have different criteria of identity associated with them. Locke was perhaps the first philosopher to grasp this point clearly, remarking that 'such as is the *Idea* belonging to [a] Name, such must be the *Identity*' (2.27.7). The criterion of identity for *trees*, for instance, is very different from the criterion of identity for *mountains*. This becomes clear if one considers how in practice one would go about settling questions of identity in the two cases. Having planted a young sapling in the corner of my garden many years ago, I might return after a long absence to find the same tree to be a large and spreading one located in a quite different position (the sapling having been transplanted at some stage). *Trees*, thus, can undergo very considerable changes of shape and position while remaining numerically the same, that is, while persisting identically through time. By contrast, it does not make much sense to talk of *mountains* undergoing radical changes of shape and position, because they are geographical features, whose very identity is partly determined by the contribution they make to the contours of a given part of the Earth's surface. If the land falls in one place and rises in another, we do not say that a mountain has *moved*, but rather that one mountain has ceased to exist and another has been created. (To be sure, we do allow 'small' changes in the shapes and positions of mountains, and this does potentially lay us open to paradox, since a long series of small changes can add up to a large change – as in the notorious paradox of the bald man. This, however, just shows that 'mountain', like many other general terms in ordinary language – such as 'red' and, indeed, 'bald' – is a *vague* term. In what follows I shall ignore problems of vagueness, important and interesting though they are.)

But what exactly *is* a 'criterion of identity'? So far I have just described it as a principle determining the conditions under which things to which the same sortal term is applicable are the same or different. It is important, I think, not to see such a principle as having a merely *epistemic* or *heuristic* status, serving to tell us what kind of *evidence* would support or defeat an identity claim concerning things of a given sort. Thus the fingerprint test, though a highly reliable guide to the identity of human beings, does not constitute a *criterion* of identity for them in the sense we are now concerned with. Rather, the criterion of identity for things of a given sort will tell us what – as Locke himself puts it – the identity or diversity of such things 'consists in'. As such, a criterion of identity is at once a *semantic* principle, insofar as it is an ingredient in the meaning of a given sortal term, and also a *metaphysical* principle, telling us about the fundamental nature of the things to which the term applies. (There can hardly be anything more fundamental to the nature of a thing than its *identity* – what makes for its sameness both at a time and over time.) More will emerge about the character of criteria of identity in later sections, where we shall examine several such putative criteria in detail.

We may conclude this section by considering an intriguing question which naturally arises at this point, namely, this: if two different sortal terms have different criteria of identity associated with them, is it nonetheless possible for both of these terms to be correctly applicable to one and the same individual thing? It may seem obvious at first sight that the answer must be 'No' – and, indeed, I believe that this is the correct answer. After all, nothing could be both a *tree* and a *mountain*, say. However, other examples are not so immediately compelling as this. One which we shall soon encounter in discussing Locke's views about personal identity is raised by the question of whether something could be both a *person* and a *man* – for Locke himself is insistent that the sortal terms 'person' and 'man' have different criteria of identity associated with them (correctly so, in my view).

Some identity theorists – known as 'relativists' – hold that it *is* possible for something to be both an F and a G, where F and G are sortal terms governed by different criteria of identity; while other theorists – known as 'absolutists' – disagree with this (see further Wiggins 1980, ch. 1). An implication of the relativist view is that it may make sense to say that an individual thing x is the *same F* as an individual thing y and yet that x is *not* the *same G* as y: for instance, that A.B. is the same *man* as C.D. but not the same *person* (see Geach 1980, p. 181). My own view (see also Lowe 1989b, ch. 4) is that this way of talking is incoherent, as I shall explain in due course. An interesting further question is whether Locke himself was a relativist or an absolutist. He sometimes *writes* as if he were an adherent of relativism, but since he never explicitly raises the issue and does not even give any clear evidence of having been aware that there *is* an issue to be settled, I am afraid that it seems impossible to provide a definite answer to this exegetical question. (For further discussion, see Chappell 1989.)

Locke on the identity of matter and organisms

One of the first applications by Locke of his important insight that different sortal terms are governed by different criteria of identity is in drawing the distinction he does between the identity conditions of what he calls 'parcels of matter' on the one hand, and living organisms on the other. An example of a parcel of matter would be a *lump of gold* or a *piece of chalk*. The general terms 'gold' and 'chalk' are known by linguists as *mass* terms, because they denote kinds of *stuff* rather than kinds of individual thing. However, given any such mass term it is possible to construct a corresponding sortal term with the aid of certain all-purpose nouns like 'piece', 'lump' and, indeed, 'parcel'. Thus we have to hand such (complex) sortal terms as 'lump of gold' and 'piece of chalk' which, like all genuine sortal terms, have both criteria of application and criteria of identity associated with their use.

Note, incidentally, an important difference between the general terms '*lump* of gold' and '*portion* of gold'. The difference is that a *lump* of gold, although *divisible* into two or more distinct lumps, does not actually *consist* of distinct lumps, whereas a *portion* of gold does (typically) actually consist of other portions of gold, which in turn consist of other such portions, and so on and on – a sequence which terminates, perhaps, in gold atoms. The consequence is that 'portion of gold' is *not* exactly a sortal term, at least in the sense that it is not possible to *count* portions of gold in a principled way, even though we do indeed presume that there is a criterion determining whether a given portion of gold is the same as or different from another. We could, however, define a *lump* of gold as a 'maximal connected portion' of gold – that is, as a portion of gold which does not consist of any sub-portions not spatially connected to one another either directly or by other sub-portions, and which is not in turn a sub-portion of any larger such portion: in short, as a 'whole mass' of gold. This is what Locke himself clearly means by a 'mass' or 'parcel' of matter. Evidently, we *can* count lumps of gold in a principled way, because any one such lump must be spatially disconnected from any other. (Two such lumps may, of course, be *contiguous*, but they cannot 'cohere' or 'fuse' without merging into a *single* lump and thereby ceasing to exist as *two* distinct lumps.)

Locke, as an atomist, presumes that parcels or masses of matter are ultimately composed of indivisible atoms of appropriate kinds, such as gold atoms. Would a gold atom itself qualify as a 'parcel of gold', if it enjoyed an existence separate from other gold atoms? The answer might be thought to be that a Lockean atom of gold would *not* qualify as a parcel or piece of gold because, *ex hypothesi*, it does not *consist* of gold (as it contains no sub-portions of gold). However, such an atom is certainly *gold* – indeed, is so *par excellence* – and is moreover *all of a piece*, so I am inclined to say that it *would* qualify as a 'piece of gold'. Be that as it may, it is important to note that atomism (whether in its modern or in its classical, Lockean form) is a speculative theory about the nature of matter rather than a necessary consequence of our ways of individuating and classifying parcels of matter: these practices are perfectly consistent with the possibility that matter of various different kinds is homogeneous throughout, defying division into 'least parts'.

This last observation raises a query, however, about the propriety of Locke's proposed criterion of identity for parcels or masses of matter. If I was right to claim in the previous section that criteria of identity are *semantic* principles, serving to convey part of the *meaning* of the sortal terms with which they are associated, and yet atomism is part of a speculative *theory* of the nature of matter rather than a conceptual implication of our existing understanding of mass terms, then surely it cannot be correct to include reference to atoms in one's statement of the criteria of identity putatively associated with the corresponding sortal terms? I think that this objection is correct, and yet not particularly damaging to Locke's proposal. His proposal is that

> whilst [a number of atoms] exist united together, the Mass, consisting of the same Atoms, must be the same Mass, let the parts be never so differently jumbled: But if one of these Atoms be taken away, or one new one added, it is no longer the same Mass or the same Body. (2.27.3)

Now if we allow that gold atoms, say, qualify as *least portions of gold*, then I think we can regard Locke's proposal as tantamount to one which appears consonant with ordinary linguistic usage, and untainted by speculative theory. This is the proposal that a parcel of gold remains the same provided only that it continues to consist of the same portions of gold, that is, *neither loses nor gains the least portion of gold.* (Of course, if atomism is false and there are no such things as 'least portions of gold', we must construe the italicised clause as meaning 'neither loses nor gains any portion of gold however small', which is indeed one legitimate reading of the words in question.) As I have just implied, I think that our existing linguistic practices are in fact reasonably well in accord with just such a criterion, in that ordinary speakers would indeed be prepared to agree that *if it could be discovered* that a portion of gold, no matter how small, had been lost from or added to a given piece of gold, this would suffice to warrant the verdict that the piece of gold existing after that operation was *not strictly the same as* the piece of gold existing beforehand. (Such speakers might also agree that in practice such small losses and additions are often undetectable, and consequently that in a 'loose' sense pieces of gold that are strictly different may often be called the 'same', with no harm done.)

It has been necessary to get as clear as possible about Locke's notion of a parcel or mass of matter and the criterion of identity he associates with this notion, in order to understand precisely why he wishes to associate a *different* criterion with sortal terms denoting kinds of living organism, like the term 'oak tree'. His reasoning is stated succinctly in the following passage:

> In the state of living Creatures, their Identity depends not on a Mass of the same Particles; but on something else. For in them the variation of great parcels of Matter alters not the Identity. (2.27.3)

Locke's point, then, is that a living organism, such as an oak tree, constantly loses and gains portions of its matter through processes of growth, metabolism and ageing, without our being in the least inclined to say, on this account, that we have strictly and literally *different oak trees* before and after such a gain or loss, in the way we *do* say just the equivalent in the case of lumps of gold or pieces of chalk. So what, then, *does* make for sameness and difference in the case of oak trees and other living organisms? Locke's answer is a little vague, perhaps, but still plausible: it is that the identity of a living organism consists in the continuance of such biological processes as are necessary to sustain its overall organisation and economy. As long as an oak tree continues to have roots, trunk, branches, and so forth, all serving their normal biological roles in furthering the life of the whole, so long does the tree continue to exist as one and the same tree – despite changes in size, shape, coloration and, most importantly, *constituent matter* (2.27.4). If, as happens in the case of organisms like amoebas, an organism splits symmetrically in such a way that each of the fission products has a 'life of its own', then, it seems by Locke's criterion, the original organism has been replaced by two new ones, implying a change of identity.

A question which we need to address here is what the relation is that obtains between a living organism, like a tree, and the parcel of matter that composes it at any given time. For we have seen that, by Locke's account, a parcel of matter cannot persist identically through the gain or loss of portions of matter, however small, and yet that a living organism can. This seems to imply that a living organism is never to be *identified* with whatever parcel of matter it is that composes it at any particular time, for the life-histories of these entities differ.

This verdict agrees with that of the 'absolutist' conception of identity mentioned in the previous section, according to which one and the same individual thing cannot have applicable to it two different sortal terms which – like 'oak tree' and 'parcel of matter' – have different criteria of identity associated with their use. And a quite general argument in favour of this claim can, indeed, be abstracted from the case just considered. The argument is just this. If a sortal term applies to an individual, then the life-history of that individual must be consistent with the criterion of identity associated with the sortal term in question. But different criteria of identity will inevitably have different implications for the life-histories of individuals to which the associated sortal terms are applicable – and since the same individual cannot have different life-histories, both surviving and not surviving some particular event (such as the gain or loss of a portion of matter), it follows that one and the same individual cannot have applied to it two sortal terms with which different criteria of identity are associated.

There is, however, an apparent awkwardness about this conclusion, as it affects things like living organisms and the parcels of matter composing them at any given time. This is that it obliges us to say that we can have at one and the same time two *different* things occupying exactly the same region of space: a tree, say, *and* a certain parcel of matter. To some this will look suspiciously like a case of double vision, and indeed of double counting. My reply is that we should recall the connection between the notion of counting and sortal terms. We do not and cannot simply count *things*, without any reference to what *sorts* of things we are supposed to be counting. If we are asked to count the *trees* in a wood, we shall – quite rightly – not include in the count the parcels of matter composing those trees at the time of counting. Similarly, if we are asked to count the *parcels of matter*, we shall not include the trees. Of course, we *could* conceivably be asked to count *both* the trees *and* the parcels of matter, and to this question we could indeed provide a correct answer by adding together the answers of the previous two questions. This would *not* be 'double counting' (which is counting the *same* thing twice), but it would certainly be a very odd and unusual procedure – sufficiently odd, perhaps, for it to strike us as something like double counting. (The oddity arises from the fact that we normally count collections of objects *all* of whose members are governed by the *same* criterion of identity.) My suggestion, then, is that it is the oddity of such a question, rather than any impropriety in refusing to identify trees with parcels of matter, that makes us feel a little uneasy about saying that we have 'two different things' in the same place at the same time.

Locke on persons and personal identity

Locke seems to have been the first philosopher to address the problem of personal identity in anything like its modern form – indeed, it was he who was responsible for setting the terms of the modern debate, and his views on the issue remain highly influential. The reason why he was able to discern a question to which previous philosophers had been oblivious is to be located, once again, in his vital insight that different sortal terms convey different criteria of identity – though he himself never uses the expression 'criterion of identity', which is of relatively recent origin, stemming from important work of Gottlob Frege in the philosophy of mathematics (see Lowe 1989a). It is this insight that leads him to make the remark: 'This being premised to find wherein *personal identity* consists, we must consider what *Person* stands for' (2.27.9).

A note of caution which needs to be sounded here is that we should not fall into the trap of supposing that, because things of different sorts have different identity conditions, there are therefore different *kinds of identity* for different sorts of thing – that the term 'identity' is itself ambiguous. Such an error, to which Locke himself may have been a little prone, is encouraged by talk of '*personal* identity', '*animal* identity', '*material* identity' and the like, as though these were different species of a genus. Rather, we should construe talk of 'personal identity', say, as talk about what *constitutes* identity in the case of persons – that is, as talk about the conditions under which a person picked out in one way (for instance, at a certain time and place) is identical with a person picked out in another way. By 'picking out' a person, I mean *making identifying reference to* a certain person, or singling out that person uniquely, whether in thought or in speech. For instance, I might pick out a person in one way as *the person to whom I am now talking*, and in another way as *the person whom I saw in such-and-such a place last week*: and then the question would be what conditions need to be satisfied for it to be the case that the persons thus picked out are the *same*. How must the person referred to first be related to the person referred to second in order for the first to be *identical* with the second? For reasons explained in the first section of this chapter, this should not be construed primarily as a question about how I can *know* whether or not such an identity obtains, but rather as one about what *has to be the case* in order for the identity to obtain.

The example just discussed involves an issue of what is called *diachronic* personal identity – that is, the identity of a person *over or across time*. And it is to such cases that most philosophical attention has been paid, not least by Locke himself. But we should not be misled by this into supposing that the problem of personal identity is one exclusively concerned with identity over time, that is, with the *persistence* or *survival* of persons. There is also the question of what makes for personal identity *at* a time – the question of *synchronic* personal identity. Such a question is posed when we ask, for instance, what determines whether or not the person performing a certain action is identical with the person having a certain thought – a question which arises in particularly intriguing form in the case of so-called 'split-brain' patients, in whom thought and action sometimes seem to come apart in strange ways (see Popper & Eccles 1977, pp. 313ff.).

Locke, we recall, starts his inquiry into the nature of personal identity by examining the meaning of the sortal term 'person'. What do we *mean* by 'a person'? According to Locke, we mean by this a 'thinking intelligent Being, that has reason and reflection, and can consider it self as it self, the same thinking thing in different times and places' (2.27.9). Thus the defining characteristics of personhood, for Locke, are rationality and consciousness, including *self*-consciousness. Here we find echoes of the views of other philosophers, but also differences from those other views. Thus, Locke's 'person' sounds rather like Descartes's *res cogitans* (literally, a 'thing which thinks'), but a crucial difference, as we shall see, is that for Descartes a *res cogitans* must be a thinking *substance*. Again, there are points of contact between Locke's 'Being, that has reason and reflection' and Aristotle's definition of *man* (or, as we should now say, *human being*) as a 'rational animal' – though, as we shall also shortly see, Locke wants to pull apart the notions of 'person' and 'animal' (but not in quite the same way as Descartes did).

Should we accept Locke's definition of 'person'? A problem here is to decide upon the status of such a 'definition'. If it were intended merely as an account of how the English word 'person' is actually understood by ordinary speakers of the language, we could settle the question of its correctness simply by consulting a reliable dictionary. But in fact a philosophical 'definition' is almost never intended to be a mere statement of how a word is currently used. If it is about usage at all, it is more in the nature of a *recommendation* – a proposal as to how an expression should be understood. Justifying such a recommendation is a matter for philosophical theory, and may involve many different considerations. Even so, like any theory, a philosophical theory – such as Locke's concerning the nature of personhood – must ultimately be answerable to certain sorts of evidence, including our commonsense intuitions or judgements concerning the matter in hand. Those judgements may not be unassailable, and indeed we sometimes find that our intuitions alter in the light of theory, but they should not be set aside without good reason. There are deep questions of philosophical method involved here which we cannot go into further now. For what it is worth, however, I shall declare my opinion that Locke is basically correct in maintaining that the proper conception of a *person* – the proper conception of what *we ourselves* are – is that of a *rational, self-conscious being*. I would only add – though I take this to be implicit in Locke's own definition – that persons are, furthermore, necessarily subjects of *perception* and authors of intentional *action*, that is, are both *percipients* and *agents*.

Does Locke's definition of 'person' help him in his quest for a criterion of personal identity? He himself clearly believes so. Having identified *self-consciousness* as the key ingredient in the proper conception of a person, Locke finds it entirely natural to conclude that personal identity is determined by the scope of self-consciousness – that 'as far as this consciousness can be extended backwards to any past Action or Thought, so far reaches the Identity of that *Person*' (2.27.9). Thus I am *identical* with myself of a week, or of ten years ago, by virtue of the fact that I still *remember* the thoughts I had and actions

I performed at those times. Intuitively appealing though this proposal is, it is deeply fraught with difficulties and paradoxes, as we shall discover in the next section. For the time being, however, we shall be more concerned to understand it and its implications more clearly.

One thing which immediately follows from Locke's definition of a person, and his attendant account of personal identity, is a separation between the concepts of *person* and *man* (or *human being*). The concept of a man is at least in part a *biological* concept, of an animal of a certain kind, with certain inalienable bodily characteristics. But Locke is insistent that no *particular* bodily form is crucial to personhood (even if the possession of *some* bodily form is necessary). This is the moral of the incredible story he tells of a certain 'rational parrot', which surprised a visitor by engaging in intelligent conversation (2.27.8). Such a creature would, by Locke's account, qualify as a person though obviously not as a *man*. Locke is adamant, consequently, that *personal* identity should not be confused with *animal* identity: that what makes for the sameness of a *person* differs from what makes for the sameness of an *animal* (including *man*). According to Locke, the criterion of identity for men is in fact just that for living organisms quite generally, and thus not significantly different from the criterion he earlier proposed for oak trees, as the following passage makes clear:

> the Identity of the same *Man* consists . . . in nothing but a participation of the same continued Life, by constantly fleeting Particles of Matter, in succession vitally united to the same organized Body. (2.27.6)

This criterion obviously has quite different implications from those of Locke's proposed criterion of *personal* identity, with the latter's focus on sameness of *consciousness* rather than sameness of 'life'.

Locke tells us some other imaginary tales (what would today be called 'thought experiments') to convince us of these differences. For instance, he asks us to imagine the 'consciousness' of a certain poor cobbler being exchanged with that of a certain prince, so that the person with the prince's body wakes up one morning remembering *as his own* various thoughts and deeds had and performed earlier by the person who possessed the cobbler's body at that time (2.27.15). We intuitively agree that the person who wakes up is the *same person* as the person who earlier had those thoughts and performed those deeds, but we obviously cannot say that the *same living human body* lies in the prince's bed as previously lay in the cobbler's bed.

At this point we may recollect our discussion in the previous section concerning the relationship between a living organism and the 'parcel of matter' composing it at any given time. We concluded that, because living organisms and parcels of matter are governed by different criteria of identity, there could be no question of *identifying* such an organism with the parcel of matter composing it. Similar considerations now appear to compel us to conclude that, if Locke is right, a person is never to be *identified* with the living organism that constitutes his or her body at any given time – for, as Locke's story of the prince and the cobbler seems to show, a person could in principle continue to exist as one and the same person despite a change in the identity of the living organism that constituted his or her body. Locke himself does not appear to be fully aware of this implication, if indeed his theory commits him to it. He often speaks in terms which sound sympathetic to a 'relativist' conception of identity, according to which the man waking in the prince's bed is the *same person* as, but not the *same man* as, the man who went to sleep in the cobbler's bed.

I shall not attempt to resolve here the question of what Locke 'really' thought about the problem just raised, though I continue to believe myself that what he *ought* to have said is that this 'relativist' way of talking is strictly incoherent, and that a *man* (understood as a kind of animal) cannot literally be 'the same person as' another man, because a man in this sense is not a *person* at all. (Of course, if by 'man' we just mean '*person* with a male human body', the latter statement is false, but by the same token we can no longer, on *that* interpretation, say that the 'man' who wakes up is *not the same man* as the 'man' who went to sleep.)

But if a person is *not* a living organism, what *is* it? Is it perhaps a Cartesian *res cogitans* – a thinking *substance*, that is (according to Descartes), an immaterial 'soul' or 'spirit'? Locke does not believe so. It is not that he denies the existence of spiritual substances – though he does famously speculate at one point that God, in His omnipotence, could have 'superadded' a power of thought or consciousness to matter (4.3.6). He thinks it likely that we have 'souls' and that thought and consciousness are properties, or 'modes', of such spiritual substances – in short, that it is our soul that thinks 'in' us. Yet he is insistent that our identity as persons does not depend, logically, upon the identity of our souls as spiritual substances. His point is that it is, he believes, perfectly *conceivable* that a single person should undergo a *change* of spiritual substance during the course of his or her existence, and equally *conceivable* that a single spiritual substance should successively serve as the soul of two distinct persons. All that is required for the first possibility is that my present soul should be *conscious of* – that is, remember – the thoughts and experiences of my past soul; and all that is required for the second possibility is that my soul should be *un*conscious of – that is, *fail* to remember – the thoughts and experiences it had when it was the soul of a previous person. Locke once again appeals to certain 'thought experiments' to convince us of these possibilities.

However, Locke's doctrine here, while congenial to those who are in any case suspicious of the Cartesian notion of a *res cogitans*, has some very odd implications. For if we allow that there *are* souls which do the thinking 'in' us, then surely we must allow that those souls are themselves *persons* in their own right, because they appear to meet Locke's criterion for personhood (they are thinking, self-conscious beings). And yet by Locke's account my soul is not the *same* person as *me*, because I could get a new one. Moreover, two quite different kinds of thing now seem both to qualify as persons – things like *my soul*, and things like *me*. These two kinds of thing have different criteria of identity. Yet we have already argued that a given sortal term, such as 'person', can have only *one* criterion of identity associated with it. The proper solution to this set of difficulties, I believe, is to reject, after all, Locke's attempt to differentiate between persons and thinking substances. Persons *are* thinking substances. But we need not therefore suppose that they are to be conceived of along Cartesian lines as 'immaterial souls'. If the notion of an immaterial soul lays itself open to sceptical doubts about whether my soul has changed overnight, or is perhaps identical with the soul of some ancient Greek (as in one of Locke's imaginary examples), then so much the worse for *that* conception of a 'thinking substance'. The best conception we can frame of a thinking substance is precisely the conception of a *person*, with *ourselves* providing paradigm examples of this category of being.

Difficulties for Locke's account of personal identity

Locke contends that '*personal identity* consists . . . in the Identity of *consciousness*' (2.27.19). But there is a problem in understanding precisely what Locke means by 'consciousness', particularly when he speaks of things 'partaking of' or 'participating in' the *same* consciousness. Indeed, I think that there is even some inconsistency in what Locke says about these matters. Sometimes he implies that it is *persons* that do or do not 'partake of the same consciousness', and as a consequence are or are not identical (2.27.19). At other times he implies that it is *spiritual substances*, or souls, that do or do not 'partake of the same consciousness', and as a consequence do or do not constitute souls of the *same person* – by analogy with the way in which material particles do or do not constitute parts of the *same animal* depending on whether or not those particles 'partake of the same life', that is, are 'united' by biological processes into a single living system (2.27.10). Most of the time, however, it makes more sense to interpret Locke according to the first of these accounts, and this is what I shall do from now on. On this view, 'participation in the same consciousness' is a relation between a person identified in one way and the same person identified in another, such as – to use Locke's example (2.27.19) – 'Socrates waking' and 'Socrates sleeping' (if indeed these *do* partake of the same consciousness and consequently *are* the same person).

But what exactly does 'participation in the same consciousness' *mean* when construed thus as a relation between persons? In *diachronic* cases – as we saw in the previous section – it is natural to understand it in terms of a *memory* relation. The waking Socrates may or may not remember certain thoughts and experiences of the sleeping Socrates. But in *synchronic* cases such an interpretation would obviously be out of place. Consider, for instance, the problems posed by so-called 'split-brain' patients, or those suffering from what is known as 'multiple-personality syndrome'. Here 'participation in the same consciousness' is better understood, it seems, in terms of some notion of the 'unity' of consciousness. 'Ordinary' people (like our-selves!) have, we suppose, a 'unified' consciousness in the sense that we are, as it were, 'jointly' conscious (or aware) of all the things of which we are currently conscious. Thus, if I am conscious of a pain in my toe, and simultaneously conscious of thinking about a philo-sophical problem, then I am conscious of *thinking of the problem while having the pain*. There is some doubt as to whether such unity is con-sistently exhibited in the case of the patients just mentioned, whence a Lockean conception of personal identity seems to imply that in con-fronting such a patient we may in fact literally be confronting *more than one person*. However, this already throws up a difficulty for the Lockean conception, if we have interpreted it correctly, because even 'ordinary' people (who are, surely, *single* persons if there *are* any!) exhibit at times some degree of disunity of consciousness, albeit a much lesser degree than that displayed by split-brain patients and sufferers from multiple-personality syndrome. We are all familiar, for instance, with the ability of people to 'divide their attention' between different tasks – such as driving a car and talking to a friend.

However, let us turn now to the still more problematic *diachronic* cases. In these, as I have just remarked, 'participation in the same con-sciousness' seems to be understood by Locke as a way of talking about *memory*. He is implying that what makes me now the same person as myself of yesterday is the fact that I now remember the thoughts, expe-riences and deeds of my earlier self. To this it is natural to object that I likewise remember what many *other* people thought, felt and did yesterday. But Locke's point would be that I *do not* in fact 'likewise' remember these, for I remember *my own* thoughts, experiences and deeds in a special way – in what we may call a 'first-person' way. I remember them, as it were, 'from the inside', as episodes undergone *by me*. By contrast, I remember events in the life of another person only in an 'external' or 'third-person' way, as episodes undergone *by some-body else*.

These observations seem quite persuasive, but we may have some doubts as to whether they can serve to explain, non-circularly, what personal identity 'consists in', since the very description of first-person memories seems to rely upon an antecedently given notion of personal identity. My first-person memories are those in which I recall some past episode in the life of a person as being one involving *myself*, as opposed to any *other* person, and this seems to presuppose that I already need a grasp of what constitutes the difference between myself and another person in order to enjoy, and recognise, distinctly first-person memories. (It is not clear just how this 'circularity' objection relates to one famously raised by Bishop Butler (1736) in the eighteenth century, and I shall not pursue the matter here.)

To this objection it might be replied that what I need in order to appreciate the notion of first-person memory is not a conception of remembering some past episode as having involved *myself*, but the weaker conception of remembering some past episode 'from the point of view', as it were, of someone involved in it – *without* any presumption that that person was *myself*. Indeed, it may be urged (and has been urged by some modern philosophers like Derek Parfit (1984)) that one could, in principle, 'inherit' first-person memories of episodes in the lives of *other people*. However, this immediately appears to create a *problem* for Locke rather than helping him out of a difficulty. For if one *can* have first-person memories of episodes in the lives of other people, then, clearly, such memory does *not*, after all, provide a satisfactory criterion of personal identity across time.

But perhaps it is possible to tread a middle course between the two alternative difficulties facing Locke (circularity on the one hand and falsehood on the other). We might urge that the 'weaker' conception of first-person memory just mooted is correct (thus avoiding circularity), but also urge, in agreement with Locke, that any past person to whom I now stand in such a relation of first-person memory is to be *identified* with me, so that it is simply *denied* that one could, even in principle, have a first-person memory of what *another* person did or experienced, as being inconsistent with the proposed criterion of personal identity.

Now, however, other difficulties loom for Locke. If it is not part of the very conception of a first-person memory that it is a memory of some past episode as one involving *oneself* – as the 'weaker' conception maintains – what is to prevent the possibility of my standing in such a memory relation to episodes in the lives of *two distinct persons* at some past moment of time? The very logic of the identity relation makes it impossible for *one* present person to be identical with *two different* past persons, and yet it is *not* apparently forbidden by the very logic of the first-person-memory relation that one present person should have such memories of episodes in the lives of two different past persons. Hence, it seems, the two relations can 'come apart', implying that the second cannot 'constitute' the former in the case of persons, contrary to the (revised) Lockean proposal.

This difficulty – that first-person-memory relations do not appear to share the same logical properties as the identity relation – crops up in connection with another objection to Locke which we shall discuss shortly, so it is worthwhile spelling out the basis of such problems more generally. *Identity* is what logicians call an *equivalence* relation, by which is meant a relation that is reflexive, symmetrical and transitive. A *reflexive* relation is one that relates a thing to itself if it relates it to anything. A *symmetrical* relation is one that relates a first thing to a second thing if it relates the second to the first. And a *transitive* relation is one that relates a first thing to a second thing if it relates the first to a third and the third to the second. *Being a brother of* is an example of a symmetrical relation (between males), because if x is a brother of y, then y is a brother of x. It might also appear to be an example of a transitive relation, implying that if x is a brother of y, and y is a brother of z, then x is a brother of z. However, that cannot strictly be so because it is not a reflexive relation – no one is a brother of *himself* – and if a relation is both symmetrical and transitive it must be reflexive. Now, according to the Lockean proposal, a given present person x is identical with a given past person y just in case x has first-person memories of episodes in the life of y. The problem, quite generally, is that the relation of first-person memory is not, like identity, an equivalence relation. It seems logically possible for x to have first-person memories of episodes in the lives of two distinct past persons y and z, but x cannot be *identical* with both y and z, because the symmetry and transitivity of identity imply that if x is identical with both y and z, then y and z are identical with each other.

But if the relation of first-person memory fails to be an equivalence relation, is this because it is not *symmetrical* or because it is not *transitive*? (We know that it could not be both symmetrical and transitive, but not *reflexive*, so it must either fail to be symmetrical or fail to be transitive.) It may seem obvious to reply that it is *symmetry* that

111

fails, because although a *present* person may remember the thoughts and deeds of a *past* person, the reverse could hardly be the case. But this reply arguably involves a simple, if understandable, confusion. What is at issue is whether a person *identified in one way* does or does not remember the doings of a person *identified in another way*. These modes of identification may indeed make reference to present and past times, but do not imply that the persons thus identified are dated items. Indeed, the notion that persons, like events, are dated items is arguably absurd and incoherent. People do indeed have dates of birth and death – that is, the events of their birth and death have dates, or are dated – but they themselves do not and are not. There is nothing absurd, thus, in saying that the person whom I met last week (a past-tense mode of identification) remembers something done by the person I shall visit next week (a future-tense mode of identification).

Be that as it may, there is in any case another important objection to Locke's memory criterion of personal identity which clearly focuses on the issue of *transitivity*. This is an objection made famous by the counter-example of the 'brave officer' presented by the eighteenth-century Scottish philosopher Thomas Reid (1710–96). Reid (1785) asks us to imagine a case in which an old general has a first-person memory of performing an act of bravery in battle as a junior officer, while the junior officer had a first-person memory of stealing apples as a boy – and yet the general no longer remembers the boyhood incident. By Locke's account, it seems, the general is the same person as the junior officer, who is the same person as the boy, but the general is *not* the same person as the boy, in direct conflict with the transitivity of identity.

Now in fact a relatively simple adjustment to Locke's account seems to enable it to overcome this difficulty. This is to replace, in Locke's proposed criterion, the relation of first-person memory by a relation which logicians would call the 'ancestral' of that first relation. The ancestral of a non-transitive relation is always guaranteed to be transitive itself. For instance, the relation of *being a parent of* is not transitive; but the 'ancestral' of that relation, namely, the relation of *being an ancestor of*, is indeed transitive. (Of course, the term 'ancestral' relates to this very example.) In order for x to stand in the ancestral of the memory relation to y, it suffices that x remembers

the deeds of someone who remembers the deeds of someone who ...
who remembers the deeds of *y* (where the gap is filled by a finite
sequence, no matter how long, of intervening clauses of the same
form). With this revision made, Locke is entitled after all to claim that
the old general is the same person as the boy.

However, I think it must be doubtful whether Locke himself
would have been happy with this revision, even though it helps to
bring his theory more in line with common sense. For he really does
seem to be quite strongly committed to the view that if you cannot currently recollect the past thoughts and deeds of some person, then you
simply are *not* the same person as the person who had and did them.
This is partly connected with Locke's belief that 'person' is what he
calls a *forensic* (that is, a legal-cum-moral) term, closely connected
with our practices of attributing responsibility and distributing rewards
and punishments. He strongly believes that a person should not be held
responsible and punished for deeds which he has no recollection of
performing (though he concedes that in practice an excessive loophole
would be created for criminals if courts always had to *prove* that a
defendant had such a recollection). Perhaps this just testifies to some
confusion on Locke's part, because one could of course agree with him
that persons should 'not be held responsible for' – in the sense of *not
be penalised for* – misdeeds which they do not recollect doing, without agreeing with him that such persons should be regarded as not
being *identical* with the perpetrators of those misdeeds, and thus 'not
be held responsible for' them in the sense of *not be regarded as the
authors of* those misdeeds. Be that as it may, I suspect that Locke's
own response to Reid's example would have been to accept with
equanimity that the general is not the same *person* as the boy, while
pointing out that the general is nonetheless the same *human being* or
man as the boy – using 'man' in a sense which does not imply adult-
hood, of course! (This admittedly invites a 'relativist' reading of
Locke's conception of identity.) That still leaves Locke with the problem of the conflict with the transitivity of identity, but my suspicion
is that Locke, who never had a very high opinion of the dictates of
logicians, would simply have dismissed this aspect of the objection
as mere sophistry. Perhaps, after all, the logicians' notion of identity
as an equivalence relation is not what *he* has in mind in talking of

'personal identity'. If so, I think his theory is mistaken, but not, as Reid would imply, simply confused.

In defence of the substantial self

What sort of a thing does Locke suppose a person or self *to be*, 'in itself'? We know, of course, what his conception of *personhood* is, from his definition of a person as a 'thinking intelligent Being, that has reason and reflection, and can consider it self as it self' (2.27.9) – in short, a rational, self-conscious subject of thought and experience. But it is one thing to define a concept of selfhood and quite another to specify the intrinsic nature and ontological status of the entities, if any, that are believed to satisfy the terms of that definition. As far as Locke's *definition* is concerned, the entities in question are merely specified as 'beings' – which is to say no more than 'entities'.

Now, in fact it emerges from Locke's text that he regards persons (with the exception of God, if He is a person) as having, strictly speaking, the ontological status of (highly complex) *modes* – remembering that a 'mode' is a quality or property of a substance. For by Locke's account, as we saw in Chapter 4 (pp. 72–3), there are, ultimately, only three kinds of substance: God, finite spirits, and material atoms. And, as we saw earlier in this chapter (pp. 106–7), Locke implies that persons are not to be identified with finite spirits or 'souls', because these could be replaced without a change of person and, conversely, there could be a change of person even without a replacement of soul. We may *have* souls, as we *have* bodies: but we *are* neither our souls nor our bodies nor the combination of the two. Rather we *are*, by Locke's account, highly complex *properties* of certain substances – probably of spiritual substances, but conceivably (as God *could* 'superadd' thought to matter) of material substances. These complex properties are *states of consciousness*, or, more accurately, complex patterns of successive and interrelated states of consciousness.

In a sense, then, what I *am*, on Locke's view, is my own conscious mental history, as far back as my current memory reaches. I am what William James (1890, ch. 10) was much later to call a 'stream of thought'. I concede that one cannot find an *explicit* endorsement, or even statement, of this view in Locke's writings – and perhaps not in any philosophical text until Hume's *Treatise of Human Nature* – but it does appear to me that Locke is committed to it, particularly in the light of his remark, made just after specifying God, finite spirits and material atoms as the only three types of substance, that 'all other things [are] but Modes or Relations ultimately terminated in [these] Substances' (2.27.2).

This view of the self as being, literally, an *insubstantial* thing, may be deeply disturbing to some, though to others it may seem liberating. But our concern now is with its intellectual rather than its emotional satisfactoriness. My own opinion is that it is ultimately an incoherent view. My objection to it is, however, quite different from any of those raised against Locke's account of personal identity in the previous section, for those objections could perhaps be circumvented by adjustments to Locke's theory in keeping with its general tenor. The objection I have in mind involves, like one of the earlier objections mentioned, a charge of circularity, but this time not one specifically directed at the notion of first-person memory. My charge is just this: that in attempting to specify the identity conditions of persons in terms of relations between the conscious mental states of persons, Locke fails to appreciate that those conscious mental states already depend for *their* identity upon the identity of the persons whose states they are, and consequently that his attempt is vitiated by circularity. Since it may not be immediately obvious what is at issue in this objection, some preliminary explanation is called for.

Let us recall that Locke's basic idea is that a person identified in one way is the *same person* as a person identified in another way just in case those persons 'participate in the same consciousness' – that is, to use a convenient modern expression, just in case those persons are 'co-conscious'. What does co-consciousness amount to, though? In a diachronic case, as we saw in the preceding section, it amounts to the fact that a person at a later time has a first-person memory of some conscious thought, experience or action which occurred to some person at an earlier time. Thus co-consciousness is a relation which holds between persons (more accurately, between a person and himself), if it holds at all, in virtue of a relation between certain *conscious states* of those persons – for instance, between a present first-person-memory state and a past thought or feeling.

But what determines the identity of particular conscious states, such as particular memories and thoughts – what is *their* 'criterion of identity'? Such states are *modes*, and as modes their identities inevitably depend upon the identities of the substances whose modes they are. Just as the particular redness and roundness of a rubber ball cannot exist without that very ball, and cannot 'migrate' to another ball, so a particular conscious state, such as a pain, belongs inalienably to whatever substance 'has' it – and *which* pain it is is determined by *which* substance has it. A pain is not an ontologically independent entity, capable of a 'separate' existence. Now, the curious feature of Locke's theory is that, while he accepts the substance/mode distinction, and accepts also that conscious states are modes, he does *not* think that they are modes *of persons*, because he does not think that persons are substances at all, strictly speaking. Rather, persons themselves are just highly complex modes compounded out of conscious states. The conscious states are, rather, modes of *finite spirits* (in all probability – barring a decision by God to 'superadd' them to matter). Hence, the identity of a conscious state will depend on the identity of the *soul* or *spirit* which 'has' it.

Thus far Locke's own theory cannot be accused of circularity, inasmuch as he holds that the identity of *persons* is determined by relations of co-consciousness between the conscious states of finite spirits, where the identity of those states is in turn determined by the identity of those spirits. For the latter, according to Locke, are *not persons*, so no circularity ensues. The problem arises, however, when we reflect upon the awkwardness of Locke's denial that spirits are persons and, still more fundamentally, the difficulty of bringing 'spirits' or 'souls' into the account at all. I have already observed (pp. 107–8 above) that it is hard to see why 'finite spirits', if they exist, should not *be persons* (for they think and feel) – and if they are, it is hard to see how there could be *Lockean* 'persons' *in addition*. If my 'soul' is a person doing all the thinking and feeling 'in' me, then how can 'I' somehow be a person different from that soul? (A modern analogue is the problem of how I can be something different from my brain if it is my brain that does 'my' thinking.) Once souls are admitted on to the scene, *they* become the prime candidates for personhood, and exclude all others, leaving us with a substantial theory of the self quite at variance with Locke's.

But perhaps we should dismiss all talk of immaterial souls in any serious account of personal identity, on the grounds that the very existence of such supposed substances is empirically unconfirmed – perhaps unconfirmable – and scientifically suspect. (Locke himself acknowledges that we are very much 'in the dark' as to the existence and nature of spiritual substances (2.27.27).) Very well, but then we can no longer make reference to finite spirits as determining the identity of conscious states: *which* state a particular conscious state is can no longer be said to depend upon which finite spirit 'has' it. However, unless we go down the disastrous Humean road of reifying conscious states, we must continue to regard their ontological status as that of *modes* – but modes *of what substance*? Locke, as we have noted, does indeed contemplate the possibility that conscious states might be modes *of matter* – and, after all, that is what a modern materialist would presumably urge (if he could countenance the existence of conscious states at all). However, Locke himself already appears to have foreclosed the possibility that the identity of a conscious state might depend on the identity of any material *body*, because he allows (as in his story of the prince and the cobbler) that a person's consciousness may be transferred from one body to another, without loss of identity.

Be that as it may, we can, in any case, put an end to all these conjectures by observing that in fact it is evident that the identity of a conscious state depends precisely upon the identity of the *person* whose state it is. *I* could no more have *your* pain or *your* thought or *your* memory than one rubber ball could have another's redness or roundness. This, however, implies that it is of *persons* that conscious states are modes, and consequently that persons are, *pace* Locke, *substances* – indeed, thinking substances. But if that is so, the whole Lockean strategy of trying to specify the identity conditions of persons in terms of relations between their conscious states is doomed to vicious circularity – as would be any attempt to specify the identity conditions of a substance in terms of relations between its own modes.

Observe, however, that in declaring persons to be thinking substances, that is, to be possessed of mental modes, we do *not* have to agree with Descartes (and, it seems, with Locke) that thinking substances are *immaterial spirits* or 'souls'. For there is nothing to prevent us from declaring that persons *also* have material modes, that is, bodily characteristics of weight and shape and the like. Only the unspoken and unproven Cartesian assumption that no substance can have *both* mental *and* material modes stands in the way of such a proposal. Moreover, such a proposal does not even require us to challenge Locke's claim that the identity conditions of *persons* differ from those of *animals* (including *man*, conceived as a kind of animal): for one may agree that a person, while necessarily having bodily characteristics of *some* sort, could in principle survive a change in such characteristics that would be incompatible with the survival of the *same animal* (perhaps even a change which involved the substitution of an inorganic, robotic body for an organic, animal body).

This is not the place to pursue this proposal any further; nor is it the place to explore alternatives to Locke's ultimately unsuccessful account of the identity conditions of persons. What can, however, be retained from Locke's theory is his valuable insight that the concept of a person is at root a *psychological* one, of a kind of being endowed with certain distinctive mental powers, centrally including rationality and self-consciousness. Where we must, I think, disagree with him is over his implicit classification of persons as *insubstantial* beings, effectively constituted by streams of conscious thoughts and feelings suitably interconnected by memory (see further Lowe 1991a and 1991b).

Action

Locke on volition and voluntary action

Locke's theory of voluntary action is an extremely interesting one, both in its own right and because of the light it throws upon more general aspects of Locke's philosophy of mind and moral psychology. But unpacking exactly what Locke wants to say about the concept of voluntary action is no easy matter, and is subject to much disagreement amongst commentators. Some of this disagreement seems to stem from the desire of some commentators not to attribute to Locke what they consider to be an untenable or incoherent theory of action. Part of my aim in this chapter will be to show that Locke *did* adhere to a theory of a sort widely held to be untenable, but that it is not in fact untenable – indeed, that it is largely correct.

Locke is a *volitionist*. That is to say, he believes that what makes an action voluntary is the involvement in it of a special kind of mental event, which may variously be called a *volition*, a *willing* or an *act of will*.

According to Locke, such a mental event is, in the broadest sense of the term, a species of *thought* (2.21.5). In modern terminology, we may say that it is an event with *intentional content*. One might be tempted to go further and say that volition or willing is a *propositional attitude*, on a par with states like *belief* and *desire*. We believe and desire *that* something is or be the case – for instance, believe that the world is round or desire that there be eggs for breakfast. But in fact I think that willing is not best construed on this model because one does not will *that* one perform a certain action, but rather one simply wills *to do* that action. The point is quite an important one because it implies that there need be no reference to *the agent* in the intentional content of a volition, and this makes it more plausible to ascribe volitions, and hence voluntary actions, to animals and young children, who may well lack any very clear conception of themselves as the *agents* of their own voluntary actions. A better model for volition is provided by the vocabulary of 'trying' – indeed, we do not go far wrong in saying that willing *is* trying. And *what* one tries is always *to do* something – for instance, to tie one's shoelaces – not *that* one tie one's shoelaces.

Locke himself sometimes characterises a volition as a 'command' of the mind (2.21.5) – that is, as a sort of self-directed imperative thought, of the form 'Do this!' But there are problems with this suggestion. For example, to obey a command one must do what is commanded, and do it *voluntarily*. Hence, by Locke's account, one must *will* to do it. But if willing to do it is *itself* just a matter of issuing a self-directed command, it looks as though it must involve the agent in a *further* act of will, and so on *ad infinitum*. This is just one example of a style of objection to volitionism – the accusation that it generates one or other kind of infinite regress – which is very common, and we shall meet another shortly. In this particular case the objection is to be met, I believe, by rejecting the 'inner command' model of volition and focusing instead on the parallel (some would say identity) with *trying*. (To be fair to Locke, he too is wary at times about using words like 'command' or 'order' to characterise volition (2.21.15).)

How is a volition to perform an action related to that action? The correct answer – which I think was also Locke's answer – is, I believe, that they are related *causally*. But we must be careful here *not* to say that the volition causes *the action*, because the volition is in fact *part* of the action, and no event can cause an event of which it is itself a part, as this would involve it in *causing itself*. In a voluntary action, we have to distinguish between the *action as a whole*, the *volition* to perform that action, and what I shall call the *result* of the volition, which is another and quite distinct part of the action. For instance, when an agent performs the voluntary action of *raising his arm*, his volition to raise his arm is one part of his action and another part is the *rising of his arm*, which is the 'result' of that volition, and a direct causal consequence of it. So *what* one wills to do – raise one's arm – is not the same as the *result* of one's willing – the rising of one's arm.

That Locke himself espoused this causal view of the role of volition is confirmed by passages such as the following:

> all our voluntary Motions . . . are produced in us only by the free Action or Thought of our own Minds. . . . For example: My right Hand writes, whilst my left Hand is still: What causes rest in one, and motion in the other? Nothing but my Will, a Thought of my Mind; my Thought only changing, the right Hand rests, and the left Hand moves. (4.10.19)

But despite such passages, this causal interpretation of Locke has been challenged, notably by John Yolton. Yolton concedes that in such passages 'Locke has used the locutions of mental causation: my thought and my volition cause my actions', but goes on to urge that 'Locke saw the absurdity in saying volitions cause actions, since . . . volitions would in turn need actions to cause them, and so on *ad infinitum*' (Yolton 1970, pp. 141–2). And in support of this Yolton refers us to the *Essay*, 2.21.25, a passage to which I shall turn in a moment.

On the face of it, perhaps, it may look as though Yolton is not in fact in disagreement with me, because I too want to deny that on Locke's view 'volitions cause actions'. But my reason for denying this is, as I explained earlier, that I think we need to distinguish between the 'result' of a volition and the action of which both volition and result are parts. Yolton, by contrast, is apparently unmindful of this distinction and simply wants to deny a *causal* theory of volition to Locke, because he believes (and believes that Locke believes) that any such theory is absurd, because committed to an infinite regress.

But what is the evidence that *Locke* believed this? Yolton directs us to the following passage:

> to ask, whether a Man be at liberty to will either Motion, or Rest; Speaking or Silence; which he pleases, is to ask, whether a Man can *will*, what he *wills*; or be pleased with what he is pleased with. A Question, which, I think, needs no answer: and they, who can make a Question of it, must suppose one Will to determine the Acts of another, and another to determinate that; and so on *in infinitum*. (2.21.25)

But in fact this passage in no wise purports to represent as absurd the idea that volitions cause what I have called the 'results' of actions – for instance, that my volition to raise my arm causes the rising of my arm. Rather, Locke is concerned here to represent as absurd the notion of a *freedom to will*, construed as involving an ability to exercise *one's will* in *determining* one's own acts of will, on the grounds that this would require us to speak of an agent *willing to will* something, and *willing to will to will* it, and so on *ad infinitum*.

Not only do I *not* think that Locke considered a causal view of the role of volition to be absurd; I think that he clearly espoused just such a view himself and moreover that such a view is fully defensible. (I shall defend it against some further objections in the next section.) Using the example of arm-raising, we may summarise Locke's position as endorsing the following equivalence:

1. An agent *A* raised his arm *voluntarily* if and only if *A* willed to raise his arm and *A*'s willing to raise his arm caused *A*'s arm to rise.

A minor adjustment to 1 is perhaps needed to overcome what is known as the problem of 'deviant' or 'wayward' causal chains (analogous to a similar problem afflicting the causal theory of perception, discussed in Chapter 3, pp. 59–60). The point is that one can perhaps conceive of abnormal circumstances in which an agent's volition to raise his arm causes his arm to rise, but only, as it were, 'by accident'. For instance, suppose that the arm is tied down to a fixed beam but some brain-monitoring device which detects a volition of the agent to raise his arm is accidentally linked up to a mechanism which causes the beam, and with it the arm, to rise. If the agent's volition caused his arm to rise by such a devious route, we should be inclined to deny that he raised it *voluntarily*, and perhaps even that he *raised* it at all. How to exclude such deviant cases by suitably modifying 1 is a problem which we shall not pursue here, unaware as Locke himself was of such a problem – though I do consider the difficulty to be a relatively minor and readily soluble one.

Another aspect of Locke's account of voluntary action which we should briefly consider is his treatment of cases of voluntary *omission* to act – what he calls 'forbearance'. Locke quite rightly includes omissions within the scope of the voluntary: one can voluntarily *omit* or *forbear* to raise one's arm when someone asks one to, for example. But a question which arises here is what, if anything, should be regarded as the 'result' of a volition to forbear to do something? It sounds distinctly odd to say that *A*'s volition to forbear raising his arm caused the *non*-rising of his arm – for there is arguably no such event as the non-rising of *A*'s arm. Non-events are not *events*, just the non-existence of certain events. But events – of which volitions are a species – cause *events*, surely: so it seems as though there is nothing for a volition to cause in a case of voluntary omission or forbearance. Locke's own view of the matter is apparent from the passage quoted earlier involving the example of the left and right hands: when one voluntarily forbears to move one's hand, one's volition causes one's hand to be in a state of *rest*. Provided one includes such states, as well as events like movements, amongst the things that events can cause, the case of voluntary omissions provides no special difficulty, it seems, for a causal theory of volition like Locke's.

Finally, there is the issue of *in*voluntary action. It is clear that Locke considered an involuntary action to be one in which no volition of the agent was causally operative (2.21.5). Thus, presumably, he had in mind such 'actions' as the blinking of one's eyes as a fast-moving object approaches one's face – sometimes called 'reflex' actions. Clearly, he was *not* thinking of cases in which, as we say, an agent acted 'against his will' – as when a bank clerk hands over money to an armed robber in response to a threat. Such actions as these are still *voluntary* by Locke's account (though no doubt *excusable*), because they involve the engagement of the agent's *will*.

Some questions and answers about volitions

One objection to volitionism – a doctrine espoused, incidentally, throughout the seventeenth and eighteenth centuries by philosophers as diverse as Hobbes, Descartes, Locke, Berkeley and Hume – is that the relationship between volitions and their supposed effects is in fact too intimate for them to play their intended role as the putative causes of those effects (see Melden 1961, ch. 5). This is sometimes known as the 'logical connection argument'. The underlying assumption – which I have no wish to challenge here – is a thesis that has been called 'Hume's principle', namely, the thesis that causes and effects are 'logically separable' or, as Hume himself would put it, 'distinct existences'. Of course, any particular cause can be *described* in a way which involves a 'logical connection' with some description of its effect – as when the cause of an event *e* is simply described as 'the cause of *e*'. But Hume's principle implies that there must always be a way of adequately characterising the cause of a given effect which does *not* make the existence of that effect a logical consequence of the existence of the cause thus characterised (and vice versa: the cause must not be a logical consequence of the effect). If the striking of a certain match caused a certain fire, I *could* describe the former event as 'the cause of that fire' – and the statement 'The cause of that fire occurred' does indeed entail 'That fire occurred.' But I could *also* describe the cause simply as 'the striking of that match', and 'The striking of that match occurred' does *not* entail 'That fire occurred.' Hence the events in question satisfy Hume's principle and can be regarded as capable of standing in a genuine causal relation to each other.

Consider now a Lockean volition and its putative effect. Adherents of the present line of objection will urge that we cannot adequately characterise the volition in any way which does not run up against Hume's principle. Let me say at once that I would agree with this objection if it were directed against the proposal that what a volition causes is the corresponding *action* of the agent: that, for example, *A*'s volition to raise his arm causes *A*'s voluntary action of raising his arm. For although '*A* willed to raise his arm' does not – or so I would claim – entail '*A* voluntarily raised his arm', I concede that

'*A* voluntarily raised his arm' *does*, according to the sort of volitionist account I favour, entail '*A* willed to raise his arm.' (That this is so is, indeed, an immediate implication of equivalence 1 of the preceding section.) But it will be recalled that the reason why I rejected this proposal is that I regard the volition as being a *part* of the action, and denied that an event could cause another event of which it was itself a part. In effect, I was thus appealing to Hume's principle myself in rejecting this proposal, for if two events are related as part to whole, they are not 'distinct existences' capable of standing in a causal relation to each other in accordance with Hume's principle.

But suppose instead that we say that what *A*'s volition to raise his arm causes is the rising of *A*'s arm. Does this still fall foul of Hume's principle? Not as far as I can see. It is true enough that in specifying the intentional content of *A*'s volition in terms of its being a volition to *raise his arm*, we are implicitly making reference to the event which is the intended 'result' of the volition – the event of *A*'s arm's rising. But, of course, mental events and states frequently do have intentional contents which carry reference to objects and events which may fail to exist or occur. Thus a hallucinatory perceptual state may have as part of its intentional or representational content that the subject is confronted by a snake or a dagger, even though no such snake or dagger really exists. In like manner, then, one may have a volition to *raise one's arm* even though no such action of arm-raising occurs – indeed, even if, as in the case of an amputee suffering from the 'phantom limb' phenomenon, there is no such arm to raise.

The possibility of an agent's genuinely performing a volition to raise his arm in the absence of the intended 'result' was convincingly demonstrated by a famous case described by William James (1890, ch. 26), in which a patient suffering from loss of kinaesthetic sensations in his arm – which was, unbeknownst to the patient, being kept under restraint – was asked to raise the arm. The patient was convinced that he had obeyed the request successfully by raising his arm, even though he had in fact failed to do so. This, I think, shows that the patient had done just what he *normally* did to raise his arm – that is, *will* to raise it – but in the absence of the normal result. Thus we see that volitions and their intended 'results', though related 'logically' in the sense that the intentional contents of the former carry reference to the latter, are not related in a way that violates Hume's principle – they are still 'distinct existences', and as such can stand in genuine causal relationships to one another, as the volitionist requires.

Another widespread objection to volitionism, which we have already encountered in the preceding section, is that it falls prey to a threat of a vicious infinite regress. The most famous version of this objection is due to Gilbert Ryle (1949, ch. 3), who was attacking volitionism as part of his onslaught against what he called the Cartesian 'ghost in the machine' – in other words, mind/body dualism. In fact volitionism need not be construed as a dualist theory, even though it is natural to construe Locke's version of it in this light. Ryle attempts to confront the volitionist with a dilemma, by asking whether or not volitions themselves are voluntary (recalling that they are, even according to Locke, *acts* or *exercises* of the mind, and so apparently candidates for the voluntary/involuntary distinction). Ryle argues that the volitionist cannot satisfactorily answer either 'Yes' or 'No' to this question. If he answers 'No', Ryle believes that he has no satisfactory explanation of why actions supposedly initiated by volitions should qualify as *voluntary*, given that the volitions themselves are *in*voluntary. If he answers 'Yes', then a vicious infinite regress appears to be under way, since by the volitionist's own account, it seems, a volition could only be voluntary by virtue of being caused by *another* volition, regarding which we could again pose the original question of whether or not *it* is voluntary.

Now we know already what Locke's reply to Ryle must be, for we saw in the preceding section that Locke thinks it absurd to suppose that 'a Man can *will*, what he *wills*' – in other words, that one volition can have another as its intended 'result'. And plausibly he is right: compare the peculiarity of talking about *trying to try* to do something. If someone is accused of having failed to try to do some task, we shall not happily accept as an excuse a claim that he did at least *try* to try to do it. So Locke cannot answer 'Yes' to Ryle's question of whether volitions are themselves voluntary, unless perhaps he were to contend that the word 'voluntary' is ambiguous and that volitions are voluntary in a sense different from that in which arm-raisings may be called voluntary. (Hugh McCann (1974) once proposed the following analogy in support of such a claim of ambiguity: when we say of most things that they are 'wet', what we mean is that they are impregnated with water, but we obviously do not mean this when we say that *water* is wet – rather, water is wet because it is what *makes* other things wet, and likewise volitions may perhaps be said to be voluntary because they are what *make* other acts voluntary. However, whatever its virtues, there is no textual basis for ascribing any such position to Locke himself.)

So Locke must answer 'No' to Ryle's question, and deny that volitions are themselves voluntary. But why should this render volitions ineligible for their intended role as the events whose occurrence as the initial part of an action is what makes that action a voluntary one? Ryle seems to be trading here upon an unspoken assimilation of volitions, construed now as *in*voluntary acts, to *other* sorts of involuntary acts, like the 'reflex' action of blinking when a hand is waved in front of one's face. *Of course*, if a volition were just like a blink, it would be hard indeed to see why we should call an action voluntary just because its initial part was a volition. But volitions *are not* like blinks. They are attitudinal mental states whose intentional contents carry reference to certain intended actions of the agent, and which are themselves products of various other cognitive and motivational states and processes of the agent – processes of practical reasoning, for example. None of this applies to blinks and other involuntary reflex actions. So this particular horn of Ryle's supposed dilemma harbours no serious threat for the volitionist.

To respond in this way is not just to ignore the so-called 'problem of free will', to which we shall indeed return below (pp. 132–6) – but it is quite proper to point out that providing an answer to the question of what it is that makes an action *voluntary*, which is the prime concern of volitionism, is an altogether different matter from providing an answer to the problem of free will, if indeed the latter problem *has* an answer. As Locke himself insists, it is one thing to describe an action as voluntary and quite another to describe it or its agent as 'free' – a point we shall explore further in the next section.

Other objections have been raised against volitionism apart from the two examined in this section, but none of them, in my view, is any more convincing. The *language* of volitionism, with its talk of 'acts of will', may seem outlandish to some philosophers who are excessively deferential towards what they take to be 'ordinary usage' or 'everyday speech'. Such philosophers may profess not to be acquainted with anything answering to volitions in their own mental experience – rather as Hume professed not to be acquainted with his 'self'. To them the volitionist may reply that it is indeed sometimes difficult to recognise something so commonplace that it is never *absent* from our experience. (Many people do not realise that they can see their own noses virtually whenever they can see anything at all – they just do not *notice* them!) The very experience of *trying* to do something, an experience we all enjoy countless times in any day, is precisely the experience of exercising the will, that is, of *volition*. It is little wonder, however, that eminent philosophers from Hobbes to Hume took the phenomenon of volition to be an absolutely uncontentious element of human psychology, for unlike some modern philosophers they were not obsessed with a desire to 'speak with the vulgar'.

Locke on voluntariness and necessity

Having explained what he understands by an action's being *voluntary* (see equivalence 1 of the first section of this chapter), Locke is next concerned to explain what it means for an action to be *free*, or for an agent to be free to perform it. The notion of freedom of action is obviously vital to moral philosophy, because we normally think it just to exculpate people for undesirable actions which they were under a necessity to perform. However, an interesting thesis which Locke is concerned to defend is the principle that, as he puts it, '*Voluntary . . . is not opposed to Necessary*' (2.21.11) – that is, that one and the same action may be performed *voluntarily* by the agent, and yet not *freely*, the agent being under a necessity of performing it. In illustration of this he offers us an example:

> suppose a Man be carried, whilst fast asleep, into a Room, where is a Person he longs to see and speak with; and be there locked fast in, beyond his Power to get out: he awakes, and is glad to find himself in so desirable Company, which he stays willingly in, *i.e.* preferrs his stay to going away. I ask, Is not this stay voluntary? I think, no Body will doubt it: and yet being locked fast

in, 'tis evident he is not at liberty not to stay, he has not freedom
to be gone. (2.21.10)

However, we shall discover that Locke's thesis is not quite so easy to
defend as he supposes, given his own definitions of voluntariness and
freedom.

Let us turn first, then, to Locke's definition of freedom, and his
correlative definition of necessity as absence of freedom. These can be
extracted from the following passage:

> so far as a Man has a power to think, or not to think; to move,
> or not to move, according to the preference or direction of his
> own mind, so far is a Man *Free*. Where-ever any performance or
> forbearance are not equally in a Man's power; where-ever doing
> or not doing, will not equally follow upon the preference of his
> mind directing it, there he is not *Free* . . . that Agent is under
> *Necessity*. (2.21.8)

Restricting ourselves to the specific example of an agent's action of
raising his arm, we may say that according to Locke the following two
equivalences obtain:

2. An agent *A* was *free* to raise his arm or not to raise it if and only
   if both (i) if *A* had willed to raise his arm, he would have succeeded in raising it voluntarily and (ii) if *A* had willed *not* to
   raise his arm, he would have succeeded in forbearing to raise it
   voluntarily

and

3. An agent raised his arm *under necessity* if and only if *A* raised
   his arm and *A* was *not free* to raise his arm or not to raise it.

Let us also recall at this point Locke's definition of voluntary action,
which led us to equivalence 1:

1. An agent *A* raised his arm *voluntarily* if and only if *A* willed to
   raise his arm and *A*'s willing to raise his arm caused *A*'s arm to
   rise.

Now, Locke's thesis that '*Voluntary . . . is not opposed to Necessary*' implies that it should be compatible with equivalences 1, 2 and 3 that an agent *A* should raise his arm both *voluntarily* and *under necessity*. But in fact it is not so easy to see that such a compatibility does obtain. For if we interpret 'not free' in 3 as meaning the absence of freedom as explained in 2, and then combine 1 and 3, what we seem to get as Locke's condition for an agent's raising his arm both voluntarily and under necessity is this:

4. An agent *A* raised his arm both voluntarily and under necessity if and only if (a) *A* willed to raise his arm and *A*'s willing to raise his arm caused *A*'s arm to rise but (b) even if *A* had willed not to raise his arm, *A* would still have raised his arm.

And, indeed, 4 looks to be a thesis that Locke would be happy to accept as capturing precisely the sort of situation that is illustrated by his example of the man in the locked room (an example to which I shall return shortly). But *is* it in fact intelligible to suppose that the right-hand side of 4 might ever be satisfied – that clauses 4a and 4b could jointly be true?

The problem is not simply that the joint truth of 4a and 4b would imply that the rising of *A*'s arm was *causally overdetermined*, inasmuch as *A*'s willing to raise his arm *caused* the rising of his arm and yet, by implication, other causal factors sufficient to produce this result without the help of *A*'s willing were also present. For one can perhaps imagine a science-fiction scenario in which a neuroscientist monitoring *A*'s motor cortex decides that if he detects a volition of *A* to raise his arm, he will allow that volition to produce its normal result – the rising of *A*'s arm – but that if he detects a volition of *A* *not* to raise his arm, he (the neuroscientist) will instead activate an electrode implanted in *A*'s motor cortex which will cause *A*'s arm to rise despite *A*'s contrary volition. However, observe that this is *not* a case in which clause 4b is satisfied. It *is* a case in which, if *A* had willed not to raise his arm, *A*'s arm would still have risen* – but it is *not* a case in which, if *A* had willed not to raise his arm, *A* *would still have raised it*. On the contrary, it is a case in which, if *A* had willed not to raise his arm, *the neuroscientist* would have caused *A*'s arm to rise, rather than *A* himself causing this. Moreover, it will not apparently help to try to modify the example by specifying that the neuroscientist, rather than just deciding to cause *A*'s arm to rise by activating the electrode, if *A* wills not to raise his arm, decides instead to induce in *A* a *volition to raise his arm* and allow *this* instead to cause the arm to rise. For this would require *A* to have *contradictory volitions*, both willing to raise his arm and willing *not* to raise his arm, and it is highly questionable whether this is possible. And even if it *were* possible, it is hard to see which volition would produce its intended effect, and why.

The foregoing discussion suggests that cases in which an agent acts both voluntarily and under necessity, as Locke conceives of these notions, must be at best extremely rare and bizarre and at worst impossible. But what then are we to make of Locke's alleged examples of such cases, such as the example of the man in the locked room, which seems quite commonplace and uncontroversial? The answer is that Locke's alleged examples do *not* in fact serve to illustrate his thesis that '*Voluntary . . . is not opposed to Necessary*', interpreted in the light of his own definitions of the notions in question. Take the case of the man in the locked room. What, precisely, is the action that the man is supposedly performing at once voluntarily and under necessity? What Locke *says* the man does voluntarily is to *stay in the room*. But what exactly does, or can, he mean by this? 'Staying in the room' may plausibly be construed as a species of *omission* or *forbearance*: but a forbearance to do *what*? Leave the room? Certainly, the man did *not* leave the room, because he *could not*. But can one properly be said to *forbear* to do something which it is *impossible* to do? Given that I *can not* leap a gap of twenty metres, it seems absurd to say that this could ever be something that I *forbear* to do. I may, of course, forbear to *attempt* to leap such a gap – but then, *attempting* to leap such a gap, though foolish, is *not* something that it is impossible for me to do.

For this reason, I think that what we ought to say, on reflection, about the man in the locked room is that what he forbore to do was *to attempt to leave the room*. He did not, for instance, go up to the door and try to open it, and failing that try to open the window instead. But if *this* is what he did 'voluntarily', then it is *not* also something which he was *under a necessity* of doing: for he *could* perfectly well have attempted to leave the room (though he would, of course, have failed in the attempt). Thus a more careful description of the case indicates that it does not, after all, provide an example of what Locke, by his own lights, understands by voluntary action performed 'under necessity'.

So what should we conclude about Locke's thesis that an action may be performed at once voluntarily and 'under necessity'? Strictly interpreted, in the light of Locke's own definitions, it appears to be of doubtful coherence and to be unsupported by the examples that Locke actually provides (see further Lowe 1986). And yet the examples do seem to illustrate *something* of interest in the philosophy of action, even if it is hard to say what it is. Perhaps they just show that an agent can be in a situation not of his own choosing but nonetheless in accordance with his desires. Given that agents cannot normally be justly blamed or praised, punished or rewarded, for being in situations not of their own choosing, we may conclude that an agent's regarding his situation as a desirable one is never a sufficient reason for holding him morally accountable for it or its consequences. But perhaps that ought to be sufficiently obvious in any case.

Locke on 'free will'

Locke's exploration of the problem – or, as he sometimes seems to regard it, the *pseudo*-problem – of 'free will' in the *Essay* is long and tortuous, apparently inconsistent in places, and ultimately somewhat inconclusive. Even so, he offers many valuable insights in the course of his discussion. Our main task in this section will be to see if we can extract a core of coherent doctrine from what he says.

Locke's initial skirmishes with the topic of freedom of the will are aimed at deflating the whole question as resting upon grammatical confusions. Recollect that he has already provided an account, examined in the preceding section, of what it is for an *action* to be 'free', and for an *agent* to be 'free' to perform an action. Roughly, by this account, an action was done 'freely' just in case, at the time of doing it, if the agent had willed *not* to do it he would have succeeded in forbearing to do it voluntarily – that is, a volition of his not to do that action would have resulted in its not being done. *Freedom*, thus, is a 'power' that agents have to do or not do some action according as they do or do not *will* to do it. But *the will* is likewise a 'power' that agents have, which they 'exercise' whenever they will to do or forbear to do some action. Hence, Locke remarks, to talk about *freedom of the will* is ostensibly to talk, absurdly, about 'whether one Power has another Power' (2.21.16). It is *agents* that have the powers of will and freedom – one of those powers does not 'have' the other.

Locke perceives, however, that this dismissive approach is rather superficial – that however much one may rightly poke fun at some sloppy ways of talking about 'free will', there *is* a genuine philo-sophical problem of great importance to be addressed here: the prob-lem of reconciling the notion of human freedom with the possibility that all aspects of our mental and physical behaviour are *causally determined* (though Locke himself never quite frames the problem in these terms). Even so, Locke's next main move is again a deflationary one, this time to dismiss as absurd the question of whether we are free to will what we will – for instance, '*whether a Man be at liberty to will which of the two he pleases, Motion or Rest*' (2.21.25). This, it will be recalled from our discussion above (pp. 121–2), is the question that Locke dismisses as absurdly giving rise to an infinite regress, saying 'they, who can make a Question of it, must suppose one Will to deter-mine the Acts of another . . . and so on *in infinitum*' (2.21.25).

Here I think we should pause a moment to reflect on the cogency of Locke's claim. Certainly, infinite regresses are to be avoided. But barely acknowledging the possibility that *one* act of will should have *another* act of will as its intended effect need not commit one to hold-ing that *every* act of will is the intended effect of another. One can allow for the 'iterability' of volition without having to concede its *infinite iteration*. (By allowing for the 'iterability' of volition, I mean allowing for the possibility of an agent's not only *willing* to do some action, but also *willing to will* to do it: this would be a 'second-order' volition, and one might want to allow higher orders too.)

My own opinion is that Locke was in fact right to imply that an agent cannot will to will to do something – but not because this is a *logically* incoherent notion, or necessarily leads to an infinite regress. Rather, I take the impossibility in question to be ultimately psycho-logical in nature. The situation is somewhat akin to that of belief. As Bernard Williams (1973) and other philosophers have pointed out, we cannot simply believe things 'at will' – I cannot simply *decide* to believe that the earth is flat, for example. This is not to say that my beliefs are completely beyond the control of my will, however, for there are various roundabout procedures which I can undertake, quite voluntarily, with a view to effecting an alteration in my beliefs. Thus I could voluntarily submit myself to some sort of 'brainwashing' process, knowing that the result would be to induce in me a belief that the earth is flat. What I *can not* do, though, is simply acquire this belief by *willing to acquire it*, in the way that I can raise my arm simply by *willing to raise it*. In like manner, now, I do not think that I can cause myself to will to do something simply by *willing* to will to do it – though, once again, I may be able to undertake, voluntarily, various procedures in the knowledge that they will very likely *result* in my willing to do a certain thing. For instance, a smoker may voluntarily undergo some sort of aversion therapy in the knowledge that at the end of it he will no longer smoke voluntarily – that is, will no longer will to smoke. But he cannot simply *will* to will not to smoke.

It would appear that although we do not ever, strictly speaking, have 'second-order volitions', our ability to *control* or *manipulate* our own volitions through various roundabout procedures in which we engage voluntarily, usually as a result of practical reasoning, is a distinctive feature of human (as opposed to animal) agency, and is importantly connected with our notions of freedom and responsibility – as modern philosophers like Harry Frankfurt (1982) have emphasised. As we shall see, Locke himself suggests something rather similar when he talks about our ability to '*suspend* the . . . satisfaction of any of [our] desires' (2.21.47).

Eventually, after some initial beating about the bush, Locke does settle down to consider the crucial 'Question, what is it determines the Will?' (2.21.29) – that is, what *causes* an agent to will to do a particular action. And, in his view, the 'true and proper Answer is . . . always some *uneasiness*' (2.21.29). He later expands on this by remarking: 'This *Uneasiness* we may call . . . *Desire*; which is an *uneasiness* of the Mind for want of some absent good' (2.21.31). Thus Locke's basic proposal is that the immediate cause of one's exercising one's will in a particular way is the prevailing balance of one's desires. If my desire to eat the cream cake lying on the plate before me is stronger than my desire to avoid putting on weight, or appearing greedy, or being impolite, or missing the bus, or whatever other conflicting desires I might currently have (more strictly, if my desire to eat it is stronger than the 'sum' of my 'contrary' desires), then, other things being equal, I shall decide to eat the cake, and do so – that is how I shall exercise my will, and the immediate cause of my doing so will be the preponderance of my present desire to eat it. As Locke himself puts it, 'the most . . . urgent *uneasiness*, we at that time feel, is that, which ordinarily determines the *will*' (2.21.40).

This quasi-mechanical picture of the immediate causal anteced- ents of volition is, it has to be confessed, not particularly satisfactory – and, indeed, Locke soon attempts to modify it. Not least amongst its difficulties is the danger of vacuity. For it is hard to see how one is to identify one desire as being *stronger* or more 'urgent' than others pos- sessed by the agent at the same time, save in terms of *its* being the desire that was acted upon. But then it becomes merely tautologous to assert that the desire which causes an agent to exercise his will in a particular way is the *strongest* of his currently operative desires. In any case, the whole idea of comparing 'strengths' of desires, of 'weighing' different 'sums' of desires against each other as if in a balance, seems to involve metaphors of dubious value, however tempting it may be to indulge in this way of talking. The danger is that it may present to us the *appear- ance* of a satisfactory explanation of action without any real substance.

As I remarked a moment ago, Locke does not stay long with this simplified, quasi-mechanical picture of desire determining the will – as indeed we see from his remarks about our ability to '*suspend* the . . . satisfaction of any of [our] desires' (2.21.47), in which he sees the real basis of human freedom:

> in this seems to consist that, which is (as I think improperly) call'd *Free will*. For during this *suspension* of any desire, before the *will* be determined to action . . . we have opportunity to . . . judge, of the good or evil of what we are going to do. (2.21.47)

The crucial feature of this point is its 'second-order' character. We saw earlier that Locke does not allow for the possibility of second-order *volitions*, strictly speaking: we cannot *will to will*. But now he *does* allow that we can, through the exercise of our will, refrain from acting upon our immediate desires in the light of what we judge to be the longer-term good – that is to say, we can at least sometimes take into account in our actions the desirability of our existing desires, which is a distinctly 'second-order' activity. It is far from clear that Locke has an adequate account of this complex business – though in that respect modern philosophers may not have made much advance upon him – but, even so, credit is due to him for not resting content with a simple, quasi-mechanical model of human action which would leave out a central feature of human freedom.

But what, in the end, has Locke to say about the compatibility or otherwise of human freedom with causal determinism? This is unfortunately just not clear, partly because he simply does not frame the question in the way modern philosophers do. It may be tempting to interpret him as a straightforward 'compatibilist', like Hume, urging that a 'free' action may nonetheless be a causally determined one whose immediate causes lie in the structure of the agent's desires, these in turn having their appropriate causal antecedents. But then we may find it difficult to accommodate within this picture Locke's talk about our ability to 'suspend' the satisfaction of our desires. As so often with Locke's philosophy, however, what he lacks in rigour and precision he makes up for in sound common sense, and the picture he presents of the psychological processes we go through in deliberating and acting may strike us as truer to our personal experience of these processes than the more mechanical pictures offered by Hume and those modern determinists who pride themselves on having a rigorously 'scientific' view of the mind's workings.

Volitionism vindicated

Throughout the preceding sections of this chapter I have expressed sympathy for Locke's talk of *volition* and *willing*, have used these terms myself, and have defended their use against some well-known objections. But still a suspicion may be harboured that volitionism is, if not an incoherent doctrine, nonetheless extravagant and speculative, without any real foundation in experience and devoid of genuine explanatory power. I think that nothing could be further from the truth, and that we literally cannot make sense of our experience of action, nor hope to explain its causal structure, without recognising the role of what we have been calling 'volitions' or 'acts of will'.

Two sorts of theory opposing volitionism need to be considered at this point; for if either is correct, all talk of 'volitions' is indeed at best superfluous. And both sorts of theory have many advocates at present (many more than volitionism has). The first sort of theory acknowledges that an adequate philosophy of action needs to recognise the distinctive causal role of certain mental antecedents to action, but holds that the mental antecedents in question can be satisfactorily classified as being mental events or states of kinds already invoked in other parts of philosophical psychology – notably, cognitive states like *beliefs* and appetitive states like *desires*. In a word, *belief–desire* psychology is, according to this approach, fully adequate to the task of describing and explaining the causal structure of action. The second sort of theory recognises that a special, distinctive vocabulary needs to be invoked to describe the causal structure of action, but holds that this vocabulary need find no place for talk of *volition* or *willing*, because it has all it needs in the form of certain more familiar terms like *intending* and *trying*. Of course, the second sort of theory *could* just be a verbal variant of volitionism if, for instance, its adherents understood by 'trying' effectively just what volitionists mean by 'willing': but although (as I have stressed earlier and will explain more fully later) there is a close relationship between trying and willing, most volitionists *and* their opponents want to distinguish between the two notions.

That the first sort of anti-volitionist theory is incorrect seems to me indisputable. Locke himself gives us an insight into why this is so (2.21.15). This is that *appetitive* states like desires – or, to use his example, *preferences* – are not, by their very nature, *executive* in character: that is to say, it is not in the very nature of a desire or a preference that a subject, barely by entering into such a state, knowingly sets in train a process geared to the realisation of the intentional content of that desire or preference. I can desire or prefer my arm to rise as strongly as may be, but merely doing so will not *make* it rise: to suppose that a desire or preference *as such* will or could bring about the realisation of its own content – 'make itself come true' – is, almost literally, to indulge in mere *wishful thinking*. (As for *beliefs*, advocates of belief–desire psychology will themselves generally insist – following Hume's lead – that belief can only ever give rise to action when it is conjoined with desire: but my point is that even the conjunction of belief with desire is not enough for action to ensue, without volition.)

A minor complication which needs to be addressed here is that volitionists typically will – like Locke – acknowledge that volitions themselves are caused by the antecedent desires or preferences of agents (or, more accurately, perhaps, by conjunctions of their desires and beliefs). But then it may be suspected that 'volitions' are a purely idle and superfluous additional link in the causal chain leading from desire to action. If desires (or desires in conjunction with beliefs) cause volitions which cause bodily movements, then desires *do* (by the transitivity of causation) cause movements – so why interpose 'volitions' at all? However, one could with as little reason criticise someone who says that sparks sometimes cause explosions which cause buildings to collapse, on the grounds that, given that sparks *do* cause buildings to collapse on those occasions, one might as well say that sparks cause buildings to collapse on those occasions without the intervention of explosions! The point is that *in order to act* agents need, in addition to belief and desire, what Locke described as a certain 'power' – the will – the exercise of which constitutes volition or willing (even though what 'determines' the will to be exercised in this or that way is desire conjoined with belief). This power can be defective in an agent, whom we may describe as being 'weak-willed' or, in extreme cases, psychologically 'paralysed'.

There are certain distinctive features of the *intentional contents* of volitions which are related to their role as 'executive' states of mind, and set them apart from cognitive and appetitive states like beliefs and desires. One, which I mentioned above (pp. 119–20), is that volitions, unlike beliefs and desires, are *not* propositional attitudes: we do not will *that* such-and-such be the case, but rather we will *to do* something – and *what* an agent wills to do must always be something which that agent conceives to be 'in his power'. That is why I can will to move my legs and *walk*, but cannot (to use Locke's own example) will to *fly* (2.21.15). As Locke rightly implies, the *scope* of the will is precisely the 'Dominion [the mind] takes it self to have over any part of the Man' (2.21.15).

Another important feature of the intentional content of volition is what we may call its *self-referential* character. When I will to do something, I will to do it as a consequence of *that* very act of will. This is why the act of willing *commits* an agent to the realisation of its content (though, of course, factors beyond the agent's control may frustrate that commitment). One cannot will *now* to do something *later*, because it is in the nature of willing to be at once the last step in deliberation and the first stage in action: in willing to do something, the doing has *already begun*. Again, Locke himself seems to acknowledge this in describing volition as 'an Act of the Mind knowingly exerting [its] Dominion' over the body (2.21.15), for this implies that a volition is part of the very action of moving the body in a certain way, and necessarily reflects this fact in its intentional content – that is, in *what* it is a volition to do.

These considerations may help to convince doubters that unsupplemented belief–desire psychology simply lacks the resources to describe adequately the causal structure of human action. But do we really need to supplement that psychology with 'volitions', or can we, as the second sort of anti-volitionist holds, make do with supposedly more familiar action-orientated notions like those of *intending* and *trying*? Let us take the category of *intention* first. Even a volitionist may want to accord a distinctive role to intentions. Intentions, like volitions, have a distinctive kind of intentional content. Often, what we intend is *to do something* (to do it *ourselves*, that is) – though we can also form an intention *that something be done* (perhaps by *someone else*). One might say, for instance, 'It is my intention that this furniture be given to my nephew on my death.' Some philosphers, such as John Searle (1983, ch. 3), have argued that intentions typically have a self-referential character, rather in the way I have claimed that volitions do. But intentions, unlike volitions, are characteristically *prospective*: they concern what we (or others) *shall do*, in the future, rather than what we *are doing* now. And in order for a prospective intention to be appropriately *acted* upon, when the due time arrives, an agent must clearly do something more than just *have formed* such an intention: he must *will* to execute it.

As against this, some anti-volitionists invoke a distinction between two different *kinds* of intention: prospective intentions and what they call 'intentions in action'. But it seems to me that the latter are probably nothing but volitions under another name. The anti-volitionist cannot claim, either, that the notion of an 'intention in action' is more familiar, or more rooted in ordinary ways of talking, than the notion of a 'volition': both are philosophical terms of art (though none the worse for that).

What about *trying*? This is certainly a notion deeply rooted in ordinary ways of talking about action. Moreover, I would be happy to concede that all willing *is*, by its very nature, trying. But I do not think that the reverse is true: not all trying is willing (though it always *involves* willing). Let me explain. As I understand the notion of trying, to *try* to do something *X* is to do something *Y* in the hope and expectation that doing *Y* will result in doing *X*. For example, my *trying* to catch a fish on a given occasion may consist in my casting a fly in the hope and expectation that doing this will result in my catching a fish. So *any* action can constitute a 'trying', if attended by appropriate hope and expectation on the part of the agent. Now, by this standard, an act of will or volition must always constitute a trying, because willing is always willing to *to do something* (else), and necessarily carries with it a hope and expectation of success. If I will to raise my arm, I do so in the hope and expectation that my so willing will result in my raising my arm. (A word of caution here: for reasons explained above (pp. 120–1), we should not think of willing to raise one's arm as causing the *action* of raising one's arm, so much as causing the *rising* of the arm – both this and the willing being *parts* of the whole action. 'Result in', as I use this expression in my characterisation of trying, should be interpreted in line with this remark, as denoting not a simple cause–effect relationship but, rather, a more complex relationship, normally involving both causal and part–whole relations.)

So although willing is always, by its very nature, trying, voluntary actions (like casting a fly) can also constitute trying – and such actions, though they *involve* willing (inasmuch as they are *voluntary*), are 'more' than just willings: they are, as it were, *successful* willings. That is why I refuse simply to *identify* willing with trying. But as for the anti-volitionists who contend that we can make do with the more familiar notion of trying *instead of* invoking volitions as a distinctive class of 'executive' mental acts, my response to them is that the notion of trying is in fact not fully intelligible independently of some antecedently given conception of volition. The point is that trying – other than when it is actually *constituted* by willing – must always be a *voluntary* action of some sort (such as casting a fly). Hence, to appeal to the notion of trying *without* appealing to volitions is tacitly to rely upon an unexplained notion of *voluntary action* – the very notion which we were attempting to analyse in the first place. In short, the commonsense notion of trying provides no adequate *substitute* for the explanatory role that volitions were invoked to fulfil. Volitions really are indispensable, as Locke saw, to any satisfactory account of the causal structure of voluntary human action.

Chapter 7

Language

Words, thoughts and things

Locke devotes a good deal of the *Essay* to the topic of language, and this may, superficially, appear to give a rather modern cast to his philosophy – for philosophers in recent decades have been almost obsessed with language, both as a supposed source of insight into perennial philosophical problems and as a particularly perplexing phenomenon which sets us apart from other intelligent creatures. But in fact Locke, in common with many other seventeenth-century philosophers, tends to see language as little more than a necessary but dangerous convenience: necessary as a means to clothe our thoughts in forms fit for others to apprehend them, but dangerous in being liable to abuse by those more concerned to persuade us by the force of their rhetoric than by the cogency of their thoughts. On this view, language can quite as well serve to disguise the *absence* of thought – even to its own utterer – as to provide a vehicle for genuine communication. Such

143

healthy scepticism is, unfortunately, too rarely to be found amongst present-day philosophers. (Locke devotes two lengthy chapters of the *Essay* to the 'abuse of words' and its remedies.)

Before we can examine Locke's own theory of language in any detail, we need to consider in more general terms precisely what we might expect a philosophical theory of language to achieve. It is, I think, a helpful starting-point to see such a theory as primarily concerned to explicate the interconnections between three quite distinct kinds of relation holding between three different kinds of item. These three kinds of item we may respectively call, with a certain degree of caution, *words*, *thoughts* and *things* – or, to avoid the danger of treating these items too atomistically, *language*, *thought* and *the world*. (Of course, on any account, language and thought are also parts of 'the world', but this is a complication which we can ignore for the time being.) Such a tripartite framework may, but *need* not, receive a 'realist' interpretation, since an 'idealist' construal – which would make 'the world' itself somehow a part of 'thought' – is also conceivable. All such 'metaphysical' considerations I wish to set aside for present purposes, however. Thus I shall not be concerned to rebut the objections of those simple-minded devotees of the deconstructionist slogan *il n'y a pas de hors-texte* (often translated as 'there is nothing outside the text') who would rebuke me for supposing there to be a world of things beyond words. Their position is simply a particularly implausible form of 'linguistic idealism'.

The fundamental relations we are concerned with may be depicted by the following diagram:

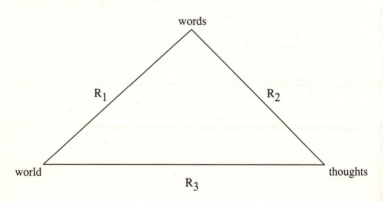

Relations of types R_1, R_2 and R_3 may be called, respectively, *semantic* relations, *expressive* relations and *cognitive* relations. Words are used by speakers to *express their thoughts* about things in the world. By virtue of having such thoughts, thinkers stand in various *cognitive* relations to things and facts in the world – for instance, they have *beliefs* about things, which may be true or false. And, finally, words and sentences themselves stand in *semantic* relations to things and facts: they *refer to* or *denote* or *mean* this or that – as, for example, a name may refer to a person, or a sentence may describe a possible state of affairs. Now, these three types of relation are at once very different from each other and yet also intimately interconnected, and one of the main tasks of a philosophical theory of language is to say something about these interconnections. Different theories of language, as we shall see, may lay different emphases on the importance of one or other type of relation – expressive, semantic or cognitive.

It is plausible to claim that it is only on account of the *semantic* properties of words (those properties they have in virtue of their semantic relations to the world) that language is a suitable vehicle for the expression of thought – though this, even if true, would still leave it entirely open whether language *acquires* its semantic properties by being used as a vehicle of thought, or whether thought itself, with the cognitive relations it involves between thinkers and the world, is wholly or partly rendered possible precisely by the uses to which speakers put words. Semantic (word–world) relations are evidently *non-natural* and in some broad sense *conventional*, as are expressive (thought–word) relations. But the status of cognitive (thought–world) relations is more controversial, depending as it does on the degree to which such relations are made possible only through the mediation of language. It seems reasonable to maintain, however, that at least *some* thought–world relations are natural and non-conventional, because it is difficult to deny that higher mammals and human infants lacking language-use are nonetheless capable of engaging in thought at some level, even if the 'higher' reaches of thought are unavailable to them. (A word of caution here: some modern philosophers of mind, such as Jerry Fodor (1976), have argued that *all* thought is encoded in a quasi-linguistic form, sometimes called 'the language of thought', or 'mentalese', and modelled on the machine code of a digital electronic computer – but it is vital to distinguish this thesis, which may or may not be sustainable, from any thesis concerning the relationship between our capacities for thought and our ability to use *public*, *conventional* languages to communicate with one another. 'Mentalese' would be neither conventional nor a means of public communication, so that even to call it a *language* is seriously misleading.)

The issue we have just been discussing (often somewhat crudely raised in the form of the question 'Does thought depend on language?') is just one of several such issues concerning relationships of priority and dependence amongst the three fundamental types of relation introduced earlier. Different theories of language and cognition may urge that one or other of these types of relation (though perhaps only within a restricted domain) is explicable in terms of one or more of the others. For example, what we might call a *cognitive theory of meaning* would attempt to explain semantic relations (R_1) in terms of expressive and cognitive relations (R_2 and R_3). On this view, words are meaningful *because* they have evolved as a means to express our thoughts about things in the world. By contrast, what we might call a *linguistic theory of thought* would attempt to explain cognitive relations (R_3) in terms of semantic and expressive relations (R_1 and R_2). On this view, thought just *is*, at bottom, the capacity to utter meaningful words about things in the world (a view often associated with some sort of *behaviourism* in the philosophy of mind). Finally, it would be possible to attempt to explain expressive relations (R_2) in terms of semantic and cognitive relations (R_1 and R_3). One might call this a *semantic theory of expression*, which would hold that words can serve to *express* thoughts just to the extent that their meaning reflects the content of those thoughts.

It would appear that none of these three types of theory in an *extreme*, reductivist form could hope to be successful. Each type of theory captures an aspect of the truth about the relationships between language, thought and the world, but if this aspect is overemphasised to the neglect of the others, confusion and absurdity will result. We have to recognise that no one whole *type* of relations – semantic, expressive or cognitive – is exhaustively explicable in terms of the other two (much less in terms of just one of them). Rather, what we must expect to find is that *some* relations of a given type are explicable in terms of certain relations of the other two types, while *other* relations of the latter two types require to be explained at least partially in terms of relations of the first type: an altogether messier but more realistic picture. Even so, this still allows scope for differences of emphasis between different theories, generating conflicts which will need to be adjudicated partly by philosophical criteria and partly by reference to empirical data of a psychological, linguistic or anthropological character.

It is in this spirit that we shall now examine the merits of Locke's approach to the nature of language and thought. But we should note at once that Locke's interest in language focuses on its *expressive* character rather than on its *semantic* relations and properties: and this serves to distance him still further from the typical concerns of present-day philosophers of language. We shall see, indeed, that – as Ian Hacking (1975, ch. 5) has also emphasised – there are grave dangers in intepreting Locke as being concerned to provide a 'theory of meaning' in anything like the modern sense, when he says: 'The use . . . of Words, is to be sensible Marks of *Ideas*; and the Ideas they stand for, are their proper and immediate Signification' (3.2.1).

Locke's ideational theory of linguistic signification

Locke, it seems clear, espouses what we may call an *ideational* theory of thought. Indeed, he speaks of thoughts as being 'made up of' ideas (3.2.1). What is less clear is precisely what we should take this theory to imply. Much earlier (pp. 19–22), I pointed to an apparent ambiguity in Locke's use of the term 'idea', whereby he sometimes seems to mean by this something close to the more recent notion of a *percept* or *sense datum* or *sense quale*, and sometimes something closer to what modern philosophers would call a *concept*. But Lockean ideas never entirely shed their sensuous character (as is hardly surprising, given Locke's strictly empiricist account of their origin). When Locke talks of *thoughts* being 'made up of' ideas, he clearly does not want to say that thinking just *is* sense-perception: but he nonetheless evidently wants to represent it as a process closely related to sense-perception. I suggest that what he believes is that thinking, at its most basic, involves an exercise of the *imagination*. I also consider that there is a good deal to say in favour of this view, despite certain limitations to which it is subject.

But what *is* 'imagination'? There is a serious danger of misrepresenting imagination as some sort of introspective scrutiny of mental images – a matter of our somehow generating a private picture show within the hidden theatre of our mind, with ourselves as the sole spectator. To regard Locke's ideational theory of thought in this light would, of course, be to impose upon him an imagistic conception of ideas as mental *objects* to which the mind stands in some special relation of awareness (the 'act–object' account that I criticised in Chapter 3). It would be altogether more helpful, I think, to interpret Locke's approach along 'adverbialist' lines (see pp. 42–7). What we can then say is that, just as in processes of sense-perception (when these are construed along adverbialist lines) there are no 'inner mental objects' but just *modes of sensing*, so in processes of imagination there are no 'inner mental objects' but just what we might call *modes of quasi-sensing*. The point of calling the modes of imagination modes of 'quasi-sensing' is to bring out the intimate relation – on a Lockean view – between imagination and sense-perception. On this view, what we do when we *imagine* some situation is to represent it to ourselves rather 'as if' we were perceiving it, exercising recognitional capacities which we have acquired in perceiving similar situations previously. I shall say more about this view of the nature of imagination later in this chapter (pp. 165–70), where I shall also argue in its defence.

Our next requirement is to clarify what Locke believes to be the basic function of language. Language, for Locke, is an artifically constructed system of *signs*. Here, however, we have to be careful to understand correctly what Locke means by the terms 'sign' and 'signification'. A 'sign', in its most general sense, is any phenomenon whose presence provides reliable evidence for the presence of some other phenomenon. For instance, dark clouds are a sign of rain. In this case, though, the sign-relation (the relation of 'signification') is a *natural* one, made possible by natural laws correlating dark clouds with rain as phenomena that are causally related. But there can also be non-natural or artificial sign-relations, generated by human or animal *conventions*. Thus removing one's hat may be a sign of respect. Locke's view of *words* is that they are artificial signs of *ideas*, and that this sign system has been generated (though not necessarily explicitly *designed*) for the purpose of communicating those ideas from one person to another – that is, for the purpose of communicating *thoughts*. A speaker's utterance of a certain word in general provides others with reliable evidence that he has, as we say, a corresponding idea 'in mind'.

Locke is adamant that a speaker can properly only use words as signs of ideas in *his own* mind, though he concedes that people often mistakenly suppose that they can use words as signs both of ideas in *other people's* minds and of *things in the world*. Here is what he says:

> But though Words, as they are used by Men, can properly and immediately signify nothing but the *Ideas*, that are in the Mind of the Speaker; yet they in their Thoughts give them a secret reference to two other things. *First, they suppose their Words to be Marks of the* Ideas *in the Minds also of other Men, with whom they communicate. . . . Secondly*, because *Men* would not be thought to talk *barely* of their own Imaginations . . . they *often suppose their Words to stand also for the reality of Things*. (3.2.4–3.2.5)

Locke castigates both of these alleged errors as 'a perverting the use of Words, [which] brings unavoidable Obscurity and Confusion into their Signification' (3.2.5).

Locke's insistence on this point may strike us as very strange, and not a little perverse itself. Surely, when we speak to others we do *not* intend, nor *should* we intend, to 'talk barely of [our] own Imaginations', but about things in the world and the thoughts of other people. However, Locke's position can be set in a much more favourable light if we recall the distinction made in the last section between *expressive* relations and *semantic* relations. If we supposed (as a modern reader is inevitably tempted to suppose) that Locke's theory of linguistic signification was intended to be a theory about *semantic* relations, then it would indeed appear that what he was offering us was a wildly subjectivist (almost solipsistic) theory of meaning, according to which what words *mean* – what they 'refer to' – are just our own ideas. This would imply, in effect, that words in a language like English have *no* public, shared meaning – indeed, that, in reality, the 'English' that each of us speaks is a quite distinct language, private to ourselves. But in fact, I suggest, Locke is concerned rather with *expressive* relations, and simply does not *have* a 'theory of meaning' in the modern sense at all.

Seen in this light, Locke's point about words properly only signifying ideas in the mind of the speaker makes perfectly good sense: it amounts to the truism that a person can only use words – primarily, at least – to express *his own* thoughts. I can, of course, *quote* another person's words, and in this secondary sense 'express another person's thoughts' – but then, so, in effect, can a parrot or a tape-recorder do this. To the extent that words are *made* to express thoughts, their *primary* use must indeed be to express the thoughts of *those who use them*: if words did not have this primary use, no secondary use such as quotation could serve any expressive purpose. To understand this point about Locke's doctrine fully, we must, however, be absolutely clear that Locke's talk about the 'signification' of words is *not* to be construed as talk about what we would now call their 'meaning' – a task made more difficult for us by the fact that 'signify' and 'mean' are nowadays often used interchangeably. Locke's claim, once again, is simply that language provides an artificial system of signs which people can exploit as publicly detectable evidence of the thoughts they are engaged in.

To defend Locke in this way is not to claim that his account of the mechanisms of linguistic signification, construed as subserving the purposes of *expression*, is completely problem-free. The *privacy* of ideas, upon which he himself insists – they are 'invisible, and hidden from others' (3.2.1) – does indeed seem to create a serious difficulty for him, though one which I believe can be resolved. The difficulty concerns the very process of *communication* which he sees as central to language use. In order for words to serve as a means of communication, Locke believes, it is

> necessary that [Man] should be *able to use* [words] *as signs of internal Conceptions*; and to make them stand as marks for the *Ideas* within his own Mind, whereby they might be made known to others, and the Thoughts of Men's Minds be conveyed from one to another. (3.1.2)

But what can Locke mean in talking of thoughts being 'conveyed from one [mind] to another'? An *idea* cannot literally migrate from one mind to another (especially on an adverbialist view of ideas). So is there not a difficulty in regarding successful communication, in the way Locke appears to, as involving the production in the *auditor's* mind of the *same idea* as that of which a word is the sign in the *speaker's* mind?

Here one might attempt to help Locke by drawing a distinction between *numerical* and *qualitative* identity or 'sameness', suggesting that what he must understand by successful communication is the production in the auditor's mind *not* of the self-same individual idea that was in the speaker's mind, but just that of an exactly (or at least closely) *similar* idea. But this suggestion does not really help Locke out of the difficulty posed by the privacy of ideas, for it is hard to see how there can be any *intersubjective*, publicly available criterion for the similarity of ideas occurring in two different minds. So how, by this account, could we ever *know* whether communication had been successful?

The difficulty can be made more vivid by reference to the notorious problem of the 'inverted spectrum'. What if the way that *red* objects look to you is the way that *green* objects look to me (with similar reversals for the other colours)? That would imply that we have quite *different* 'ideas' of red and green, and thus that the idea of which the word 'red' is the sign in *my* mind is not at all similar to the idea of which that word is the sign in *yours* – and yet we would apparently never be able to *discover* this difference, because we are in complete agreement with each other over which *things* we call 'red' and which 'green'. But does this not therefore show that success in communication *cannot* be supposed to consist in the production in the mind of the auditor of ideas similar to those in the mind of the speaker – indeed, does it not show that what 'ideas' people 'have in mind' when they use words to communicate with one another are *quite irrelevant* to their success or failure in communication?

The first point that needs to be made in response to this objection is that Locke clearly did *not* in fact think that success in communication requires the production in the auditor's mind of ideas similar to those in the mind of the speaker. For, in the course of criticising what he takes to be the common but *mistaken* belief that a speaker's words can be signs of ideas in another person's mind, Locke says the following:

> [Men] *suppose their Words to be Marks of the* Ideas *in the Minds also of other Men, with whom they communicate*: For else [they suppose] they should talk in vain, and could not be understood, if the Sounds they applied to one *Idea*, were such, as by the Hearer, were applied to another, which is to speak two Languages. But in this, Men stand not usually to examine, whether the *Idea* they, and those they discourse with have in their Minds, be the same. (3.2.4)

Here Locke is by implication rejecting the model of successful communication suggested earlier on his behalf, though he is conceding that it is a model we may be strongly tempted to adopt – because we may be tempted to suppose that two speakers can only be said to be speaking the *same language* if it enables them to communicate in accordance with this model. However, sameness of language is a *semantic* relation – a matter of words having the same *meaning* for both speaker and hearer – and I have already suggested that Locke's theory of linguistic signification is not in this sense a theory of *meaning*.

What Locke *does* understand by successful communication is a matter I shall turn to in a moment. Before that, it is worth remarking that he himself was fully aware of the 'inverted spectrum' problem and discusses it briefly in another part of the *Essay*, in the following passage:

> Neither would it carry an Imputation of *Falshood* to our simple *Ideas*, *if* by the different Structure of our Organs, it were so ordered, That *the same Object should produce in several Men's Minds different* Ideas at the same time; *v.g.* if the *Idea*, that a *Violet* produced in one Man's Mind by his Eyes, were the same as that a *Marigold* produced in another Man's, and *vice versa*. For since this could never be known . . . neither the *Ideas* . . . nor the Names, would be at all confounded. (2.32.15)

Locke goes on to surmise that such radical differences probably do *not* in fact occur, but the crucial point is that *he himself* recognises the issue as quite irrelevant to the question of whether people can use words successfully in communication with one another.

We might commend Locke for his good sense in recognising this fact, but still wonder how he can now escape the charge that any reference *at all* to 'ideas' in the minds of speakers and hearers is irrelevant to a proper account of what constitutes success in communication. But in fact he can escape this charge very easily. He does not have to give up his ideational theory of thought, or his account of communication as the 'conveying' of thoughts, provided 'conveyance' is understood appropriately. All he has to say is that communication is successful when the idea produced in the mind of the auditor is *relevantly related* – in a sense I shall explain in a moment – to the idea of which a given word is the sign in the mind of the speaker. What this 'relevant relation' is can best be explained by means of a simple example. Suppose I am describing to you over the telephone some flowers that I can see in a vase next to me, and I describe them as being 'red'. For my description of the flowers as 'red' to serve successfully in 'conveying' my thought about their colour to you, what is required, I suggest, is that *you* should associate with the word 'red' just such an idea of imagination as would correspond to *your* colour percept of these very flowers if *you* were able to see them. Whether *your* ideas and percepts are 'similar' to *mine* is indeed quite irrelevant: what is crucial is that *each of us* should associate with the word 'red' an idea of imagination similar to *our own* colour percept of objects endowed with the same particular colour, such as red. Thus, what constitutes success in communication *does* involve reference to the 'ideas' of speakers and hearers, but requires a much more sophisticated and complex account of the proper *relationship* between those ideas than is suggested by the simple 'similarity' model rejected earlier. I shall discuss this new model in more detail below (pp. 165–70). What we need to stress at the moment, however, is that the *privacy* of ideas creates no problem for the new model, since it invokes no *interpersonal* standards of comparison between ideas. And that Locke himself is committed to something like the new model, rather than the simple 'similarity' model, is clearly evidenced by his response to the 'inverted spectrum' problem.

Locke's theory of abstraction

Locke's theory of abstraction is a theory which he advances in order to explain how the *general terms* in a language play the distinctive roles they do. General terms fall into two major classes (recall the opening section of Chapter 5), the first embracing *sortal* and *mass* terms – like 'horse' and 'gold' respectively – and the second embracing adjectives like 'white', 'just' and 'human', to which we may add what are sometimes explicitly called *abstract* nouns – such as 'whiteness', 'justice' and 'humanity' – which are formed from those adjectives.

If, as Locke maintains, 'All Things, that exist, [are] Particulars' (3.3.1) and '*General and Universal*, belong not to the real existence of Things; but *are the Inventions and Creatures of the Understanding*' (3.3.11), then why do we have general terms in language at all? If this were understood as a question as to why language does not just consist of names for particular things, it would be a silly one: for names alone cannot suffice to make a language. A language needs the resources wherewith to construct *sentences*, and sentences are never merely strings of *names*: we require in addition *predicative* expressions, such as *verbs* and *adjectives*. But if our question is construed more sensibly as asking why, in addition to verbs and adjectives and names for particular things, languages contain *general names*, then it is certainly one deserving of serious attention – especially if, like Locke, one does not believe that the role of general names can be to name *general things*, that is, things that are not 'particulars'. (What would a 'general thing' be, if it existed? One traditional answer is that it would be a *universal*: something that can, unlike a particular, be wholly present in many different places at once – as the colour *red* is sometimes thought to be. Locke, because he denies the existence of universals, is often called a 'nominalist', though this is a term which can be misleading: I prefer to call him a 'particularist'.)

Locke offers three reasons why languages contain general names (3.3.2.–3.3.4): (1) that there are too many distinct particulars for each to receive its own proper name; (2) that different speakers are acquainted with, and thus have proper names for, different particulars, and yet still need to converse with each other about particulars known to only one of them; and (3) that we need to be able to convey *general* knowledge about the world, which requires expression in the form of general statements like 'Gold is valuable' and 'Horses are mammals.' The point of reasons (1) and (2) is that we use general names in constructing terms for particulars which either lack proper names of their own or whose names we do not know – terms like the definite description 'the sword Napoleon wore' and the demonstrative noun phrase 'that man' (the general names in these cases being 'sword' and 'man' respectively). All three of Locke's reasons for the inclusion of general names in language seem cogent ones, even for a 'particularist'.

We must recall, though, that for Locke the basic function of words is to *signify ideas* in the minds of speakers, in order to facilitate the communication of thoughts between speakers. So his next two questions must be: what sort of ideas do general terms signify, and how do we acquire those ideas? His answers are that the ideas in question are *abstract general ideas* and that we acquire them by a process of *abstraction from experience*. Before we attempt to examine that process, as Locke conceives of it, it is vital to appreciate that when Locke asserts that general terms signify abstract general ideas, he is not forgetting his dictum that 'All Things, that exist, [are] Particulars.' Any abstract general idea must itself be a *particular*, whether we regard it as a particular mental 'image' or – as I would prefer to – as a particular 'modification' or 'mode' of a thinker's mind, in accordance with the 'adverbialist' approach. If a speaker uses the general term 'gold' on two different occasions, each time it must signify a numerically distinct abstract general idea in the speaker's mind – though Locke would presumably expect these particular ideas normally to be closely similar, or even exactly similar, to one another. So ideas are not 'general' in the sense of being general *things* (universals) which can be wholly present at more than one place and time.

Abstract general ideas, as Locke conceives of these, are best characterised as the supposed products of the process of abstraction, a process which Locke attempts to illustrate by examples but never succeeds in defining at all exactly. One such illustration is provided in the following passage:

> [Children], when time and a larger Acquaintance has made them observe, that there are a great many other Things in the World,

that in some common agreements of Shape, and several other Qualities, resemble their Father and Mother . . . frame an *Idea*, which they find those many Particulars do partake in; and to that they give . . . the name Man. . . . And *thus they come to have a general Name*, and a general *Idea*. Wherein they make nothing new, but only leave out of the complex *Idea* they had of *Peter* and *James*, *Mary* and *Jane*, that which is peculiar to each, and retain only what is common to them all. (3.3.7)

The suggestion thus is that the process of abstraction consists in our comparing our ideas of various particulars which we encounter in experience, noting their similarities and differences, ignoring the latter and retaining in mind only the former (the similarities) as a sort of pattern or template, which we may then go on to employ in classifying further particulars that we meet: and these patterns or templates are our *abstract general ideas*. Thus one's abstract general idea of a *man* will include the idea of a body with a head, two arms and two legs, but will not include the idea of any specific colour, since we find in experience that particulars having such bodies can vary enormously in coloration.

How seriously can we take Locke's proposal as a contribution to what would nowadays be called human cognitive psychology? Is there any empirical evidence to suggest that he was right in contending that we construct such mental 'templates' (my term, not Locke's)? Despite the many philosophical objections which, as we shall see in the next section, have been raised against Locke's theory, there is in fact some support to be found for it in empirical psychology. In recent years psychologists like Eleanor Rosch have claimed that we deploy what are sometimes called 'prototypes' or 'stereotypes' in classifying and naming objects, citing in support of this evidence that subjects are quicker to name objects more closely resembling the appropriate stereotype than those which differ from it in marked respects (see Lakoff 1987, ch. 2). For instance, when presented with a series of pictures of animate and inanimate objects, and asked to name which are birds, subjects regularly identify robins and sparrows as birds more quickly than they do penguins and ostriches – the suggested explanation being that the former are much closer in appearance than the latter to the stereotypical bird. But it is also possible that such differences in reaction times could be explicable in terms of so-called 'connectionist' models of pattern-recognition, which would *not* appear to imply that subjects classify objects by somehow 'matching' them against stereotypical representations (see Bechtel & Abrahamsen 1991, ch. 4). Such models lack that implication because they suggest that mental 'representations', to the extent that they exist at all, are 'widely distributed' across a neural network which simultaneously stores many other representations exploiting the same connections between units of the network, so that on this view there would be no isolable psychological entity corresponding to a Lockean abstract general idea of, say, a bird. Interesting though these speculations are, to pursue them further would take us too far afield. Suffice it to say that current empirical psychological data and theories seem to leave it an open question at present whether Locke's approach is tenable at that level.

It will be recalled from our discussion of 'real' and 'nominal' essence in Chapter 4 (pp. 78–83) that Locke holds that the 'nominal essence' of a sort or kind of things is nothing other than the abstract general idea which our name for that sort or kind signifies. Thus the nominal essence of gold would be a complex idea including, perhaps, the ideas of a yellow colour, a shiny surface, hardness to the touch, ductility, malleability and so forth. We have remarked (pp. 82–3) on the views of some modern critics of Locke, like Hilary Putnam, who urge that Locke was wrong to suppose that the meaning of the term 'gold' consists in such an abstract general idea, or that such an idea is what determines which things are rightly to be regarded as specimens of the kind gold. Putnam's position is concisely summarised by his well-known slogan '"Meanings" just ain't in *the head*!' (Putnam 1975, p. 227). But here we should recall the distinction we drew earlier in this chapter (pp. 144–7) between *semantic* and *expressive* properties and relations. Locke was not, it seems, proposing abstract general ideas as the *meanings* of natural kind-terms like 'gold', in anything like the sense in which a modern semantic theory construes 'meaning'. He was concerned, rather, with the psychological processes underlying our use of a term like 'gold' to express our thoughts about that substance, and with our capacity to recognise things as being what we call 'gold'. Seen in this light, there may be less conflict between Locke and Putnam than the latter might suppose. For Putnam himself invokes the notion of 'stereotypes' to explain our psychological recognitional capacities, and thus arguably makes much the same use of them as Locke himself makes of his similar notion of 'abstract general ideas'. Just how much real conflict remains when we distinguish their different conceptions of what a theory of language should seek to explain is not altogether clear.

Problems with abstract general ideas

Locke's theory of abstract ideas has been the target of philosophical criticism and ridicule almost from its first appearance, one of his foremost critics being his fellow empiricist George Berkeley. Some of these criticisms are stronger than others, and some miss their mark by misconstruing Locke's position. I shall discuss the criticisms under four main headings, as follows: (1) problems of *inconsistency* and *indeterminacy*; (2) the problem of *individuation*; (3) problems with *resemblance*; and (4) the problem of *recognition*.

The first set of problems involves the charge that abstract general ideas conflict with either or both of two fundamental logical laws: the *law of non-contradiction* (that nothing can both have and not have a certain property) and the *law of excluded middle* (that everything must either have or not have a given property). The conflict with the first law, certainly, almost appears to be conceded by Locke in a famous passage, in which he speaks of the general idea of a triangle as one 'wherein some parts of several different and inconsistent *Ideas* are put together' (4.7.9) – a passage which is pounced upon by Berkeley in the Introduction to his *Principles of Human Knowledge* (13). For Locke actually says that, with regard to certain properties like obliqueness and equilaterality, the general idea of a triangle must both *have* and *not have* these properties – 'it must be neither Oblique, nor Rectangle, neither Equilateral, Equicrural, nor Scalenon; but all and none of these at once' (4.7.9). (A complication here is that Locke should plainly exercise some caution, in any case, in saying that an *idea* of a triangle has properties possessed by *triangles*: though, given his contention that our ideas of 'primary qualities', including shape, *resemble* those qualities (see pp. 55–9), perhaps he should indeed be taken at his word in this passage.)

I think that the best we can do on Locke's behalf at this point is simply to dismiss the passage just mentioned as being unrepresentative of his considered opinion concerning abstract general ideas. In many other passages (such as the passage from *Essay*, 3.3.7 quoted in the previous section), Locke makes it plain that he understands abstraction solely as a process of *excluding* or *leaving out* ideas that are represen- tative of *some but not all* of the things that are grouped together as belonging to the same sort or kind by virtue of their agreement with a given abstract general idea. Only ideas representative of *all* those things will be included, such as that of *trilaterality* in the case of tri- angles. This is the reason why, for instance, no specific idea of *skin colour* is included in the abstract general idea of a man, according to Locke.

However, this now leaves Locke with the problem of *indeter- minacy*, and the threatened conflict with the law of excluded middle: for now he seems to be implying that the general idea of a triangle will neither *have* nor *lack* equilaterality. To this it might be replied that he is only committed to saying that the general idea of a triangle will not *have* equilaterality, not that it will also not *lack* it. But then we must consider what he should say about the property of being *scalene* (having sides all of different lengths): clearly, he should say that the general idea of a triangle does not have this property either – and like- wise for the property of being *isoceles* (having just two sides of equal length). But if a three-sided figure has sides *neither* all of which have *different* lengths, *nor* only two of which have the *same* length, then it seems to follow logically that it must have sides no two of which differ in length, and hence that it cannot *lack* the property of being *equilat- eral*. So Locke does indeed appear to be committed to saying that the general idea of a triangle neither has nor lacks the property of equilat- erality. And the problem then is that the law of excluded middle seems to condemn as incoherent this implication that the general idea of a triangle can just be *indeterminate* as to the relative lengths of its sides.

I think that the only sensible way out of this apparent difficulty for Locke is to draw a clear distinction between those properties that are properties *of ideas themselves* and those properties that ideas *represent things as having.* This is a distinction which always needs to be carefully drawn for representations, of which ideas are supposed to be a sub-class. Consider, for instance, the following stick-figure sketch of a man:

The properties of the line-drawing itself are perfectly determinate: one can measure the various lengths and angles of the lines involved as precisely as one likes. But when we ask whether the picture represents a man facing *towards* us or facing *away* from us, we can give no principled answer. We cannot say *either* that it represents a man who *is* facing towards us *or* that it represents a man who is *not* facing towards us. A *man* must indeed either be facing towards us or not facing towards us, of course, but a *representation* of a man need not *represent* him either as doing so or as not doing so. There is no conflict here with the law of excluded middle, either as regards properties of the representation or as regards properties of the thing represented – and yet we can still describe the representation as being 'indeterminate' as regards the direction in which the man who is represented is facing. Note, too, that although the lines in the picture which represent the man's *arms* are perfectly *straight*, this does not imply that the man's arms are represented as being perfectly straight as well. Similarly, then, three straight lines of determinate lengths may serve to represent a triangle without necessarily representing the triangle as having sides with just those lengths, or even as having sides with lengths in the same proportions as the lengths of those lines. (This solution to Locke's apparent difficulty bears some resemblance to Berkeley's own view, suggesting that the difference between their positions may not have been as great as Berkeley supposed – for I think it quite possible that Locke himself at least sometimes thought of abstract general ideas in the way suggested here.)

I do not believe that this way out of Locke's apparent difficulty necessarily involves saddling him with an 'imagist' conception of ideas (so we should not take the stick-figure drawing too literally as a model for an abstract general idea). And in further defence of Locke we can point out that perception itself – from which abstract general ideas are supposedly generated – is a *selective* process: when observing an object we notice certain of its properties, but with regard to others we may neither notice that it *does* have them nor notice that it does *not* have them. Thus there is no reason why we should not recognise a shape as being a triangle while simply *not attending* to whether or not its sides are equal in length: and so to the extent that Lockean abstract general ideas are supposed to be what explain our perceptual recognitional capacities, their 'indeterminacy' (in the acceptable sense just defended) seems to be an entirely appropriate feature of them.

The remaining criticisms of abstract general ideas I shall deal with more briefly, since the problems of inconsistency and indeterminacy are those most commonly raised. What I have called the problem of *individuation* is just this. Locke supposes that we *classify* objects as being of this or that *sort* or *kind* by noting their agreement or disagreement with certain abstract general ideas which we have formed through our experience of particular objects. But this presupposes that we can *notice* particular objects – single them out perceptually from other objects – altogether independently of being able to recognise them as being objects of any general *sort* or *kind*. And that seems highly questionable. Of course, I may be able to single out an object as being an *animal*, say, while not yet having any idea as to what *kind* of animal it is: but 'animal' itself is a kind-term, so this by no means shows what Locke apparently needs to show, namely, that I can single out an object simply as a mere *something*, without any sortal classification of it at all. If I *cannot* do this – as I for one believe to be the case – it inevitably follows that Locke's thesis that all abstract general ideas are formed from our experience of particulars must be mistaken. The conclusion would then have to be that at least some abstract general ideas are *innate*, namely, those which even a newborn infant must deploy in its earliest feats of perceptual discrimination, whereby it singles out some objects for attention amidst others, in what William James (1890, I, p. 488) called the 'blooming, buzzing confusion' of its first experiences. But the doctrine of innate ideas, as we saw in Chapter 2, is one to which Locke is implacably opposed. Here, then, is a potential source of tension in his position.

The next area of difficulty for Locke's theory of abstract general ideas centres on his commitment to 'particularism' (or 'nominalism') – his view that 'All Things, that exist, [are] Particulars' (3.3.1). Because there are, for Locke, no real universals – no entities that are wholly present in many different places at the same time – he believes that our sorting of things under general names cannot reflect our perception of any features in them that are literally *common* to all and only those things that are classified under the same name, such as 'gold', or 'horse', or even 'red'. The things that are red do not literally possess some identical universal quality which is wholly present in each and every one of them. Rather, qualities themselves are particulars, so that the red quality of one object can never be numerically identical with the red quality of another object. But now the problem is why we should even apply the same name, 'red', to all these different qualities – and likewise with other general names, such as 'horse' and 'gold'. (There is even a difficulty in saying that we *do* apply the 'same' name to each, since names too must be particulars.) Equally there is a problem as to how a single abstract general idea can represent all these diverse particulars that are classified under the same name.

Sensibly enough, Locke does not wish to imply that our classificatory procedures are entirely arbitrary and so, like many 'nominalists', he appeals to perceivable *resemblances* between particulars:

> I would not here be thought to forget, much less to deny, that Nature in the Production of Things, makes several of them alike: there is nothing more obvious, especially in the Races of Animals. (3.3.13)

Thus any two *horses* probably resemble each other more closely than any horse resembles any member of another animal species. Locke's theory would seem to imply that such resemblances between objects are ultimately reducible to resemblances between their particular qualities, such as the particular shapes of two different horses.

Various problems can be raised for what is often called 'resemblance nominalism'. One is that in saying that two particulars 'resemble' one another, it is always necessary to specify *in what respect* they do so – for instance, in respect of *colour*, or *shape*, or *size* – and this threatens to reintroduce what appears to be talk of *universals*. Another problem, made famous by Bertrand Russell (1959a, p. 55), is that if the resemblance nominalist is to adhere consistently to 'particularism', then he must say that the resemblance which one particular has to another can never be numerically *the same resemblance* as any resemblance which that second particular has to a third – so that a problem arises as to why we group certain *resemblances* together as 'similar', a problem which cannot be resolved simply by repeating the original strategy of the resemblance nominalist at the level of resemblances themselves. (Russell concludes that there would have to be at least *one* real universal, *resemblance* – so we might as well admit others too.) Finally, it is often pointed out that *any* two particular objects chosen at random will inevitably both resemble each other in infinitely many different ways *and* be dissimilar from each other in infinitely many different ways. Most of these similarities and dissimilarities will strike us as utterly trivial and insignificant if they are brought to our attention (for instance, the fact that this sheet of paper and the front door of my house are similar in shape), but what is it that determines our criteria of *significance* in making such judgements of triviality? We can hardly have learned to construct such criteria on the basis of *experience*, since what is at issue is precisely how we manage to *experience the world selectively*, by noticing some similarities while ignoring many others. This argues once again for some *innate* component in our cognitive apparatus (perhaps what W. V. Quine (1960, pp. 83ff.) has called pre-linguistic 'quality spaces'), quite forbidden by Locke's empiricist precepts.

Locke seems oblivious to these problems concerning resemblance, but together they seem to imply that his particular combination of nominalism and empiricism is doubtfully tenable.

The final problem for Locke's theory of abstract general ideas that I want to mention is what I called earlier the problem of *recognition*. This has to do with the fact, emphasised in the previous section, that abstract general ideas themselves are, for Locke, *particulars* (whether particular mental 'images' or particular modifications of thinkers' minds). The problem is that Locke appeals to abstract general ideas to explain how we recognise objects as belonging to one or other general sort or kind – for instance, how a child recognises an individual it encounters as being a *man* (as opposed, say, to a *horse*). Locke's answer is that we perform such feats of recognition by noticing the 'agreement' of newly encountered objects with the abstract general ideas we have already formed from past experience. As he puts it, we

> make abstract general *Ideas*, and set them up in [our] mind, with Names annexed to them, as Patterns, or Forms . . . to which, as particular Things existing are found to agree, so they come to be [regarded by us as] of that Species. (3.3.13)

The model suggested here is of abstract general ideas functioning rather like patterns in a wallpaper pattern-book: to know what sort of thing we are confronted with, we compare it with a pattern in our mental pattern-book. But the patterns (abstract general ideas) are *themselves particulars*, so how do we recognise *them* as being of a certain sort or kind? How do I recognise the abstract general idea with which I am comparing a newly encountered object as being an abstract general idea *of a man* (as opposed to one *of a horse*, say)? It looks as though Locke's theory of recognition generates a vicious infinite regress.

On Locke's behalf I think we could reply that the pattern-book model, though suggested by Locke's own remarks, is not in fact essential to his thesis that recognition is mediated by abstract general ideas. It would indeed be fatal for his theory if he had to suppose that we need to *recognise* and *classify* our own abstract general ideas before we can deploy them as 'patterns' whereby to recognise and classify the objects we encounter in our experience of the world. But he need not suppose this, it seems to me. If an analogy is sought, a better one than the pattern-book might be that of the automatic vending-machine, which 'recognises' a coin because the coin matches a slot inside the machine: the machine does not require a *further* mechanism to 'recognise' *the slots*, so that it can 'compare' a particular slot with a particular coin in order to determine whether they match. Rather, the slot which matches is the one which the coin goes through. Locke, it seems, ought to say that the 'matching' of newly encountered objects to abstract general ideas is similarly an 'automatic' process, unmediated by further processes of 'recognition'. How such a model might be actually implemented in the human mind or brain is, however, more a matter for empirical psychology than for philosophical speculation.

A neo-Lockean view of language and thought

How much of Locke's ideational theory of language and thought can be salvaged from the attacks that have been made on it by subsequent philosophers? A good deal more, I believe, than is commonly supposed, provided we do not make the mistake of assuming that he is offering a theory of *meaning*, in anything like the modern sense. The questions which he *does* address are important and often neglected ones, and his answers have considerable plausibility, even if only limited application.

Locke's concern with the nature of thinking is not so much with what would now be called the problem of its *content* as with what we could term the problem of its *medium*. The problem of content (or 'intentionality') is the problem of what makes a given thought a thought *about* this or that worldly object or state of affairs. It is not that Locke has nothing at all to say about this problem. Clearly, he thinks that our thoughts get to be about objects and their qualities by virtue of consisting of *ideas* which 'represent' those objects and qualities. He even has the rudiments of a theory of representation, one of whose ingredients (in the case of the representation of primary qualities) is a notion of 'resemblance'. But none of this is worked out in any detail, and it is open to a good many objections. Probably what is needed is a much more sophisticated account of the *causal* relationships between objects and ideas than Locke provides. Causal theories of content, whereby thoughts get to be 'about' objects by being suitably causally related to them, are in vogue at present (see, for example, Fodor 1990), and one could probably graft aspects of some of these modern proposals on to Locke's rudimentary account.

The problem of thought's *medium* is the problem of what we think 'in', and Locke's answer is that we think *in ideas*. One might suppose that this problem, far from being neglected in modern times, has received a good deal of attention, notably in the form of recent speculation about the existence of a 'language of thought', or 'mentalese', modelled on the machine-code of a digital electronic computer (see Fodor 1976). Nor has this theory gone entirely unopposed – many cognitive psychologists urging that at least some of our cognitive processes involve operations on 'images', which are said to be 'scanned' and even 'rotated' by subjects in various experimental situations (see Block 1981). This may sound very like what Locke is proposing. But really that is not so. These modern psychological theories are theories of how information is encoded and processed in the human brain, and may be said to focus on the issue of whether the brain functions more like a 'digital' or an 'analogue' computer. Locke's concern, rather, is with how thought presents itself to our *consciousness* – that is, with what some philosophers would call the 'phenomenology' of thought processes. By contrast, there is no suggestion, on the part of adherents of the 'language of thought' hypothesis, that the lexical elements of that supposed 'language' are items presented to us in consciousness.

In this context it is important to grasp that the 'language of thought' hypothesis is quite different from the proposal sometimes made that we think 'in words' – and not only because the 'words' of the latter proposal are words of an ordinary natural language, like English. The point is that the latter proposal, as it is commonly understood, is a proposal concerning how thought presents itself to consciousness (as is seen by the fact that its proponents typically think that it is supported by evidence from *introspection*). It is worth pointing out, indeed, that this proposal that we think 'in words' – understood as implying that thought presents itself to consciousness in the form of *imagined discourse* or 'inner *saying*' to oneself' – overlaps at least partially with Locke's own thesis that we think 'in ideas', differing from his in limiting the 'ideas' in question to *auditory* ones related to the perceived *sounds* of words. Seen in this light, a major weakness of the proposal that we think (exclusively) 'in words' is that if it is allowed that thinking may present itself to consciousness as imagined *discourse*, it is hard to see why it should not equally be allowed to present itself as imagined activities of many other kinds.

As may now be gathered, the way I construe Locke's thesis that our thoughts are 'composed of ideas' is as the proposal that thinking – or, at least, a certain central form of thinking – crucially involves *processes of imagination*. On this view, thinking at its most basic very often simply consists in our imaginatively constructing or reconstructing various situations – situations of types with which we first become familiar in *perception*. Thus Locke's thesis forges a strong link between the conscious aspects of perception, thought and imagination. Introspection (a perfectly legitimate source of evidence in the present context) confirms the existence of this linkage. Consider, for example, how one's consciousness is modified when one is asked by a stranger to provide information about how to get from one place to another in a town with which one is familiar: typically, one resolves the problem by *imagining* how one would make the journey oneself, reporting to the stranger on the various turns to be made and buildings to be passed as one imagines oneself taking those turns and passing those buildings. This process of imagination *is* a process of 'thinking' – a way of excogitating the solution to a problem – but it is not a process of imagined *discourse* or 'inner saying'. In that sense, it is a wholly *non-discursive* mode of thinking: not a matter of *describing* to oneself the various turns to make and buildings to pass, but simply one of imagining *making* those very turns and passing those very buildings. And when one then *reports* those imagined movements to the stranger using speech, one is not simply speaking out loud words which one has already said inwardly to oneself, but rather using those words to communicate the results of one's imaginative exercise. This, it seems to me, is the central core of truth in Locke's doctrine that words are 'signs of ideas' in the mind of the speaker.

Locke's doctrine has been received critically partly because his purposes have been misunderstood and partly because the doctrine itself has been absurdly caricatured. He has been represented as advocating an impossibly subjectivist semantic theory which naively posits discrete mental 'images' as the (unavoidably private) *meanings* of individual words: as though the meaning of the word 'cat', as uttered by a particular speaker, is a private mental picture of a cat floating before the mind's eye of the speaker, and the meaning of the sentence 'The cat is on the mat' a more complex picture in which a ghostly mat is mentally drawn underneath the cat-image. Such an absurd theory is, of course, only too easy to knock down. The critic gleefully inquires: what, then, is the meaning of the sentence 'The cat is *not* on the mat'? A mental picture of an unoccupied mat? But how in that case would the meaning of that sentence differ from that of the sentence 'The *dog* is not on the mat'? The proper answer is (a) that Locke probably does not have (and certainly need not have) an imagistic conception of ideas; and (b) that he is not, in any case, offering a theory of linguistic *meaning* in the modern sense, but a theory of how language can serve to convey the results of our constructive exercises of the imagination. (Just for the record, though, it is worth pointing out that imagining that the cat is not on the mat is phenomenologically quite distinct from imagining that *the dog* is not on the mat, just as *perceiving* the one situation is phenomenologically quite distinct from perceiving the other. This has no bearing on questions of linguistic *meaning*, but it does show that non-discursive thought about negative states of affairs is perfectly possible.)

Why must thought have a 'phenomenology' at all – why must we think 'in' a medium? Well, perhaps not *all* thought is like this – perhaps a good deal of thought goes on at a level that is quite inaccessible to our consciousness. We have all had the experience of the answer to a problem simply 'popping into our mind' unbidden. But unless at some stage something *does* 'come into one's mind' – present itself to consciousness – it is hard to see how we can properly talk of *thought* going on at all. A race of beings *never* experiencing the presentation of thoughts in consciousness could hardly be called a race of *thinking* beings at all, however 'intelligent' their behaviour might be. (Perhaps lower animals and advanced computers are like this; given the connections between perception, thought and imagination, such a race of beings would in all probability have to lack any phenomenal awareness – qualia – in *perception*, too.) As to the even deeper question of how a race of beings like ourselves, capable of experiencing consciously presented thoughts, can have evolved, this seems still to be an unanswered mystery.

One difficulty for this neo-Lockean view of language and thought still needs to be addressed, and that is the problem of *privacy* (recall our mention of this at pp. 150–3). This is emphatically *not* the problem raised by devotees of Wittgenstein under the heading of the so-called 'private language argument' – for that is supposedly a problem about *meaning* (see Wittgenstein 1953, 269ff.). Still, there *is* a *prima facie* difficulty for Locke created by the fact that we can only ever be aware of the ways in which *our own* processes of perception, thought and imagination present themselves to consciousness. How, then, can I ever really succeed in conveying to another, in language (or in any other way), the results of my own exercises of imagination? We saw the beginnings of an answer to this problem earlier (p. 153). The purpose of language as an intersubjective vehicle of thought is not, impossibly, to ensure that my auditor succeeds in *reduplicating* in his own mind my non-discursive acts of imaginative (re)construction – that, for instance, the stranger asking me for directions succeeds, upon hearing my words, in imagining the twists and turns of the journey precisely as *I* do. Success consists, rather, in my enabling him to imagine the journey in such a way that, as he attempts to follow my instructions, he will recognise what he *perceives* as corresponding appropriately to what he *imagined*. My words, if successful, should enable him to *anticipate in imagination* what he will subsequently *recognise in perception*. (The fuller and more accurate my description is, the more detailed this anticipation may be.) Thus, what needs to be secured is not a similarity between how *he* imagines the journey and how *I* imagine it – a similarity which, even if it exists, is apprehensible by nobody – but rather such a similarity between how he first imagines and then perceives the journey as corresponds to the similarity between how I first perceived it and then remembered it in imagination.

Using language, we can enable others to imagine for themselves situations which we can imagine because we have encountered them at first hand. Think, for instance, of how a good football commentator in a radio broadcast enables his listeners to imagine the game pretty much as it is happening – that is, pretty much as they would *see* it happening if they were in the commentator's location. Locke is surely right to imply that this is one of the most valuable services that language provides. It liberates human beings from reliance upon their own perception and memory, enabling them to recapitulate the experience of others in their own imagination. None of this need be taken to imply, though, that there are no reaches of thought that are inaccessible to the non-discursive imagination. Plausibly, for example, much mathematical and scientific thinking is inescapably symbolic, and this extends to our thinking about measures of time and space. (One could hardly have the thought that tomorrow is Tuesday without access to modes of linguistic representation.) At the same time, we should not underestimate the scope of the imagination, and the possibilities for thought that it may confer even upon languageless animals and human infants.

Chapter 8

Knowledge

Intuition and experience

Locke's tripartite division of knowledge by reference to its sources in *intuition*, *reason* (or 'demonstration') and *experience* is a traditional one, widely adopted by other seventeenth-century philosophers. But he combines it with the somewhat peculiar and obscure doctrine that knowledge *consists in* our 'Perception of the Agreement, or Disagreement, of any of our *Ideas*' (4.3.1). This seems at best a way of characterising certain examples of what he calls 'intuitive' knowledge, and is difficult to extend, without considerable strain, to other areas of knowledge. The kinds of examples in question are those provided by Locke in passages such as the following:

> sometimes the Mind perceives the Agreement or Disagreement of two *Ideas* immediately. . . . And this . . . we may call *intuitive Knowledge*. . . . Thus the Mind perceives, that *White* is not *Black*, That a *Circle* is not a *Triangle*, That *Three* are more than *Two*, and equal to *One* and *Two*. (4.2.1)

The 'ideas' of white and black would seem to 'disagree' just in the sense that one cannot perceive a surface as being, at one and the same time, both black and white, just as one cannot perceive it as being both red and green – though whether this 'cannot' expresses a merely psychological impossibility, or something stronger, is open to debate. Such a 'disagreement' is not apparently a *logical* disagreement, in the sense that a *formal contradiction* can be derived from the statement '*S* is both black and white', when suitable definitions of 'black' and/or 'white' are provided: for, according to Locke, our ideas of black and white are simple and therefore unanalysable – a claim which does indeed have considerable plausibility. 'White' plainly does not *mean* 'not black', since red is neither black nor white. Nor does it mean 'not black nor any chromatic colour', for – even if we could non-circularly define 'chromatic colour' – grey is neither black nor white nor any chromatic colour. Nor does it mean 'not black nor grey nor any chromatic colour' – since a transparent surface can come under none of these descriptions and yet not be white either; and so it goes on.

Notice, however, that even as soon as we come to Locke's *second* example of 'intuitive' knowledge – that a circle is not a triangle – we no longer have an irreducible disagreement between simple, unanalysable ideas. A *triangle* may be defined as a plane figure bounded by three straight lines, and a *circle* as a plane figure bounded by a curved line which is everywhere equidistant from a central point – and given further axioms and definitions of Euclidean geometry it would indeed be possible to derive a formal contradiction from the statement '*F* is both a circle and a triangle.' Even so, Locke would obviously maintain – again with considerable plausibility – that our 'perception' of the 'disagreement' between the ideas of a circle and a triangle is 'immediate', rather than being grounded in a demonstration from those axioms and definitions. The same applies to his third, arithmetical example that three equals one plus two: no proof of this from the axioms and definitions of arithmetic could make us any *more* assured of its truth than we are by simple reflection upon the meaning of the statement itself. (Indeed, we are *less* certain of those axioms and definitions than we are of such simple arithmetical truths as that three equals one plus two.) That some things are indeed known to us by 'intuition', as Locke suggests, certainly appears to be at least a truth about our psychological condition – though whether it reflects anything special about the status of the *objects* of that knowledge seems altogether more debatable.

Why are some things knowable by us 'intuitively' – such as that a circle is not a triangle – but others only 'demonstratively', by inference from other things – such as that any triangle whose base is the diameter of a circle and whose opposite vertex lies on the circumference of that circle is right-angled? Locke himself says that the reason why we do not know intuitively that, for instance, the three internal angles of a triangle equal two right-angles is that

> the Mind being willing to know the Agreement or Disagreement in bigness ... cannot by an immediate view and comparing them, do it ... Because the three Angles of a Triangle cannot be brought at once, and be compared with any other one, or two Angles. (4.2.2)

But it is far from evident that this is not just a psychological limitation on our part, which could be overcome by other intelligent beings. Might not 'demonstrable' truths, such as those just cited, be as 'obvious' or 'self-evident' to some minds as it is to ours that three equals one plus two?

Once this thought strikes us, however, and we are led to realise that the intuitive self-evidence of a proposition is not an intrinsic property of the proposition itself but rather a status it has only relative to the mind of the knower, we may come to query the reliability of intuition as a supposed source of knowledge. Might there not be beings – benighted, indeed, by *our* standards – for whom it was 'obvious' and 'self-evident' that a circle may be a triangle and three equal to two plus two? Locke's 'psychologistic' approach to knowledge as being a matter of our *perception* of agreement or disagreement between our *ideas* inevitably invites such sceptical and relativistic challenges. At the same time, it makes for a degree of tension with his own repudiation of the doctrine of innate ideas (see Chapter 2). For if the obviousness *to us* (human beings) that a circle is not a triangle is a reflection of our own psychological make-up, which might not be duplicated in other species of intelligent creatures, this seems to give succour to the innatist thesis that the basic elements of our conceptual repertoire and their general organisation within our cognitive economy is fixed prior to and independently of our subsequent experience: that the human mind is not, at birth, the 'yet empty Cabinet' (1.2.15) that Locke claims it to be.

So much for knowledge by 'intuition'. As for knowledge by *reason* (that is, by logical demonstration or proof), Locke supposes, again in line with the prevailing tradition of his time, that each step in a chain of demonstrative reasoning must be perceived as intutively certain, as must the initial premises:

> *in every step Reason makes in demonstrative Knowledge, there is an intuitive Knowledge* of that Agreement or Disagreement, it seeks, with the next intermediate *Idea*, which it uses as a Proof. ... By which it is plain, that every step in Reasoning, that produces Knowledge, has intuitive Certainty. (4.2.7)

Clearly, any doubts we have about the status of 'intuition' as a source of knowledge will extend to the status of 'demonstration', on this account of reasoning. Just how adequate Locke's conception of reasoning is will be something we examine further below (pp. 182–6).

Locke's final category of knowledge, knowledge by 'sensation' – that is, by *experience* – of the existence of things other than ourselves, is especially difficult to accommodate with his official characterisation of knowledge as the perception of the agreement or disagreement of our ideas – for the simple reason that, in sensation, the idea ostensibly produced in us by an 'external' object does not appear to stand in any relevant relation of 'agreement' or 'disagreement' with other *ideas* we have, so much as a relation of 'agreement' or 'disagreement' *with external reality*: and this is a relation which we cannot be said to 'perceive' in any sense in which we may be said to perceive relations of 'agreement' or 'disagreement' *amongst our ideas*. The danger is that we may allow this consideration to persuade us (as it plainly has persuaded some of Locke's critics) that Locke's theory of sense-perception, coupled with his theory of knowledge, condemns his system to vitiation by an insoluble 'veil of perception' problem. As I explained in Chapter 3, I think that it is in fact a mistake to suppose that Locke's system is inherently any more vulnerable to this kind of sceptical problem than is even the most explicit form of 'direct' realism. In defending Locke on this score I have no wish to endorse his official doctrine as to the *nature* of knowledge – that it consists in our perception of the agreement or disagreement of our ideas – but I do want to support not only his causal theory of perception but also his commonsense insistence that sense-experience *does* constitute a reliable source of knowledge concerning the existence and, to some extent, the properties of external objects, as when he says:

> *The notice we have by our Senses, of the existing of Things without us*, though it be not altogether so certain, as our intuitive Knowledge . . . yet it is an assurance that *deserves the name of Knowledge*. If we persuade our selves, that our Faculties act and inform us right, concerning the existence of those Objects that affect them, it cannot pass for an ill-grounded confidence: For I think no body can, in earnest, be so sceptical, as to be uncertain of the Existence of those Things which he sees and feels. (4.11.3)

Perhaps what Locke needs in order to give his confidence a satisfactory theoretical underpinning is what would today be called an 'externalist' account of empirical knowledge, whereby states of knowledge are states produced by reliable mechanisms interacting causally in appropriate ways with the objects of knowledge (see Dancy 1985, ch. 9). If our 'Faculties' are such mechanisms, then their products – such as our perceptual judgements – qualify as states of knowledge by such an account, *irrespective* of whether or not those states are attended by a subjective apprehension of their 'certainty'. However, writing as he was at a time at which an 'internalist' conception of knowledge was dominant, not least through the influence of Descartes, Locke could hardly have been expected to make such an alternative, 'externalist' account his official doctrine.

Reality and truth

Some passages from the *Essay* – as when Locke says that 'the Mind knows not Things immediately, but only by the intervention of the *Ideas* it has of them' (4.4.3) – make Locke look very much like an 'indirect' or 'representative' realist, trapped behind the infamous 'veil of ideas'. But, as I have emphasised in Chapter 3, it is much more helpful to think of the 'way of ideas' as Locke's method of explaining how we have *access* to knowledge of the real world rather than as a stumbling-block to such knowledge: 'ideas' are our *bridge* to reality, or *window* upon it, not a veil or wall which screens it off from us. And, after all, no account of our knowledge of things outside us, however 'realist' and however 'direct', can place those things themselves literally inside our minds or heads. (Nor would it help us to know them any better if they *were* there.) Knowledge of things beyond us has to be mediated in *some* way by the impact which those things have on us – and the form of that impact will inevitably be conditioned not only by the nature of the things themselves but also by *our* nature and by the nature of our relationship to the things in question. Any account of knowledge which attempted to defy these constraints would have to be either anti-realist or else non-naturalistic – indeed, *super*natural. Locke is to be commended, not criticised, for grasping this fact and being prepared to work through its consequences. One of those consequences is the recognition that our knowledge of reality is inescapably limited by the nature of our situation. Reality must transcend what we can know of it: to deny that is to deny that it is really reality.

But not *every* aspect of reality need transcend what we can know of it: to suppose that it must is to avoid both anti-realism and supernatural realism only at the expense of falling into the absurdity of *transcendental* realism or 'noumenalism', as Kant did. (This may seem an odd accusation, since Kant is usually described – not least by himself – as a 'transcendental *idealist*'; the point, however, is that his 'transcendental idealism' is only a rejection of what I have just called *supernatural* realism – the view that we can have a knowledge of reality which is completely unmediated by any transactions between that reality and ourselves – whereas he does contend that there really is a world of things 'as they are in themselves' which is utterly unknowable to us, which is what *I* mean by 'transcendental realism'.) Locke's position of *naturalistic realism* – as we may call it – is arguably the only sane and stable philosophical position to adopt, and the only serious question that needs to be addressed is not whether he was right to adopt it but whether his particular account of precisely what it is that we *can* know about reality strikes the right balance between scepticism and over-optimism. If anything, I think he is unduly pessimistic about our prospects for knowledge of reality.

In response to his own question, as to how the mind shall know that its ideas 'agree with Things themselves' (4.4.3), Locke answers as follows:

> I think there be two sorts of *Ideas*, that, we may be assured, agree with Things. ... The first are simple *Ideas*, which since the Mind ... can by no means make to it self, must necessarily be the product of Things operating on the Mind in a natural way ... and so ... represent to us Things under those appearances which they are fitted to produce in us. ... *Secondly, All our complex* Ideas, *except those of Substances*, being *Archetypes* of the Mind's own making ... *cannot want of any conformity necessary to real Knowledge*. (4.4.3–4.4.5)

Locke's point about simple ideas is, it must be conceded, not entirely convincing – first because it seems question-begging to contend, as Locke does, that these could not be products of the mind's own operations and, second, because, even granting that they are produced in us by the operation of 'external' things, it may be queried whether they need correspond to unitary properties of those things, as opposed to a great variety of heterogeneous properties having the same effect on us in different circumstances. Thus, when Locke asserts that

> the *Idea* of Whiteness, or Bitterness, as it is in the Mind, exactly answering that Power which is in any Body to produce it there, has all the real conformity it can, or ought to have, with Things without us (4.4.4)

it may be objected that, for all we know, what makes one object look white or taste bitter to us is utterly different from what makes another object do this. Indeed, modern colour science *does* tell us that precisely this is so as far as perceived colours are concerned (see Hardin 1988). Lights with very different mixtures of wavelengths can all *appear* exactly the same hue to a human observer. However, curiously enough, the very fact that this is now empirically well established shows that, if anything, Locke was *too modest* in his claim about the knowledge we can have of the powers of objects to produce simple ideas in us.

We are not restricted to knowing those powers *only* by way of the very ideas in question, since by drawing more widely upon observation and experiment, we can develop well-confirmed theories to *explain* how objects produce sensory effects in us. Of course, we should not criticise Locke for failing to anticipate just how successful science could be in this regard, writing as he was at a time when the scientific revolution had barely begun.

The second class of ideas concerning which Locke believes that we may be assured that they 'agree with Things themselves' is that of '*All our complex* Ideas, *except those of Substances*'. This may sound as though it is a wildly optimistic claim – until we see what it really amounts to. The examples he gives are of such ideas as the complex mathematical ideas of a rectangle or a circle, and complex moral ideas such as those of justice and temperance, remarking:

> The Mathematician considers the Truth and Properties belonging to a Rectangle, or Circle, only as they are in *Idea* in his own Mind. For 'tis possible he never found either of them existing mathematically, *i.e.* precisely true, in his Life. But yet the knowledge he has of any Truths or Properties belonging to a Circle ... are nevertheless true and certain, even of real Things existing: because real Things are no farther concerned ... than as [they] really agree to those *Archetypes* in his Mind. (4.4.6)

So Locke's point is that in the case of a complex idea like that of a circle, and the properties which circles are conceived of as having according to that idea, the 'direction of fit' – to borrow a useful expression developed by John Searle (1983, p. 7) – is not *from ideas to the world* but rather *from the world to ideas*. That is to say, we are not under an obligation to show that our idea of a circle conforms to how circles are in reality: rather, whether something existing in reality has the form of a circle depends on whether it conforms to our idea of that shape. Similar considerations apply in the sphere of moral ideas.

As far as geometry is concerned, Locke's contention is no longer as acceptable as it may have appeared in his own day. We are now familiar with the fact that there are many consistent alternatives to Euclidean geometry: geometries in which, for instance, the three internal angles of a triangle do *not* sum to two right-angles. Locke may be right in supposing that there are, say, truths of Euclidean geometry which obtain, and can be known to obtain, independently of how things are in the real world. But nowadays we are faced with a question, unthinkable to Locke, of *which* geometry, of all those that are *mathematically* possible, best describes the metrical properties of objects located in physical space and time. This *is* an empirical question, involving the idea-to-world direction of fit. Whether anything similar can be said of ideas in the moral sphere is less clear, but arguably it can.

Why does Locke make an exception of our complex ideas of *substances*? Locke explains this as follows:

> to have *Ideas* of *Substances*, which, by being conformable to Things, may afford us *real* Knowledge, it is not enough, as in Modes, to put together such *Ideas* as have no inconsistence. . . . But *our Ideas of Substances* being . . . referred to *Archetypes* without us, must . . . be taken from something that does or has existed. . . . Herein therefore is founded the *reality* of our Knowledge concerning *Substances*, that all our complex *Ideas* of them must be such, and such only, as are made up of such simple ones, as have been discovered to co-exist in Nature. (4.4.12)

Locke's point, then, is that in the case of substances the 'direction of fit' is from ideas to the world, not vice versa. Our idea of gold should conform to the properties of something existing in the real world: but whether certain properties *do* co-occur in nature is something which we can only hope to ascertain by observation, lacking as we do (or as in Locke's time we did) any knowledge of the 'real essences' of substances which would serve to explain why some properties occur together while others do not. Locke accordingly makes only a very modest claim about our ability to acquire real knowledge of substances, but does not deny it altogether:

> our *Ideas* being thus true, though not, perhaps, very exact Copies, are yet the Subjects of *real* . . . *Knowledge* of them. Which . . . will not be found to reach very far: But so far as it does, it will still be *real knowledge*. (4.4.12)

Here Locke is, again, at once too optimistic and too pessimistic. He is too optimistic because he does not anticipate the problem which Hume was to make of induction – that is, the problem of extrapolating from our observation of the co-occurrence of certain properties in certain instances to a conclusion that those properties *regularly* occur together in nature. On the other hand, he is too pessimistic in that he did not anticipate – through no fault of his own – the degree to which empirical science *is* capable of penetrating to the 'real essences' or internal constitutions of substances, with the aid of advanced experimental technology and sophisticated methods of analysing observational data.

Finally, a word about Locke's theory of *truth*, if indeed it can be called a 'theory'. He himself seems to consider that there is nothing of substance to be said in terms of truth that is not already said by him elsewhere in terms of 'real knowledge'. Insofar as truth is a property of *sentences*, it is parasitic upon the truth of the *thoughts* which sentences are used to express, and the latter – 'mental truth', as Locke calls it – is nothing other than real knowledge:

> When *Ideas* are so put together, or separated in the Mind, as they, or the Things they stand for do agree, or not, that is, as I may call it, *mental Truth. . . . Truth of Words* is . . . the affirming or denying of Words one of another, as the *Ideas* they stand for agree or disagree: And this . . . is twofold. Either *purely Verbal*, and trifling . . . *or Real* and instructive; which is the Object of that real Knowledge, which we have spoken of already. (4.5.6)

Most modern philosophers tend to explain the notion of knowledge in terms of a prior notion of truth; in Locke the direction of explanation seems to be the reverse of this.

Reason, probability and faith

According to Locke, belief or opinion – which he contrasts with *knowledge* – may be grounded either in *probability* or in *faith*. Since, by Locke's account, the scope of our knowledge is 'very narrow' (4.15.2), in most everyday concerns we have to rely on probability, which is mere 'likeliness to be true' (4.15.3), rather than certainty. One frequently reliable ground of probability is *testimony*, on which we depend for a very large proportion of our firm beliefs, even in those matters which are capable of demonstration. Thus Locke gives an example of how a non-mathematician may firmly, and quite properly, *believe* that the three internal angles of a triangle add up to two right-angles because a mathematician 'of credit' has told him that this is so, though it is only the mathematician who *knows* that it is so, having constructed a proof or demonstration of that proposition (4.15.1). By contrast, in some matters of religion in which intuition, reason and sensation cannot provide us with knowledge, we may justifiably ground our belief in (what we take to be) divine revelation, and assent of this sort Locke calls *faith*. He is emphatic that, rightly understood, reason and faith do not stand in opposition to each other (both, he assumes, being gifts of God), but he is very critical of exaggerated claims of the scope of revelation:

> Whatever GOD hath revealed, is certainly true; no Doubt can be made of it. This is the proper Object of *Faith*: But whether it be a divine Revelation, or no, *Reason* must judge; which can never permit the Mind to reject a greater Evidence to embrace what is less evident, nor allow it to entertain Probability in opposition to Knowledge and Certainty. (4.18.10)

In all of these matters, Locke was broadly representative of the enlightened intellectuals of his time. The divisions he makes between knowledge and belief, and between reason, probability and faith, are standard ones for his time, and not so very different from standard epistemological distinctions that are still drawn today. Perhaps, though, the biggest gulf between his usage and that of present-day philosophers arises from his much more restrictive application of the term 'knowledge', as describing only that of which we are certain:

> And herein lies the *difference between Probability* and *Certainty*, *Faith* and *Knowledge*, that in all the parts of Knowledge, there is intuition; each immediate *Idea*, each step has its visible and certain connexion; in belief not so. That which makes me believe, is something extraneous to the thing I believe. (4.15.3)

Today we would regard it as very odd to say that we do not *know* that the earth is not flat, that the sun is millions of miles away from us or that Napoleon lost the Battle of Waterloo – yet, by Locke's standards, we cannot be said to 'know' these things, however justifiably assured we may be of their truth, whether through testimony or through scientific or historical research. Thus Locke is apt to sound unduly sceptical to modern ears. But though – as I explained in the previous section – I think he *was* too pessimistic about the scope of human knowledge, we should not misconstrue as scepticism a view which merely deploys the term 'knowledge' in a more restrictive sense than would be acceptable today. What *we* mean by saying that we 'know' that the earth is not flat is perhaps not so very different from what Locke would mean by saying that we 'believe' this, with a high degree of probability. At the same time, we should not be *too* lenient on Locke on this account: for, as I remarked earlier (pp. 174–5), there are grounds for supposing that his 'internalist' approach to knowledge, which is partly responsible for the connection he insists upon between knowledge and certainty, is not, ultimately, a fruitful one.

From these more general epistemological concerns, I want to turn now to an issue concerning which I think Locke does have something distinctive and important to say, and this is on the nature of *reasoning*. It was, indeed, not uncommon in the seventeenth century for opponents of Scholasticism like Locke and Descartes to pour scorn on 'syllogising', that is, upon the formal Aristotelian system of syllogistic logic that had been refined (some would say corrupted) over several hundred years at the hands of mediaeval scholastic philosophers and logicians. The general criticism was that these exercises in formal logic were utterly sterile and incapable of advancing our scientific understanding of the world in any respect. In science, *mathematical* methods had begun to prove vastly more productive than appeals to the substantial forms, essences and syllogisms of the Aristotelian approach. But Locke's criticisms of 'syllogising' go deeper than this merely practical point of utility, and have some bearing on important issues in the psychology of reasoning which are much under debate today.

To understand the significance of Locke's criticisms, we need to be clear about the nature of the syllogistic method. A syllogism is an argument consisting of two premises and a conclusion, each having one of four possible forms. These forms are 'All *S* are *P*', 'Some *S* are *P*', 'Some *S* are not *P*' and 'No *S* are *P*', where *S* and *P* are, respectively, any *subject term* and any *predicate term*. Such terms are (normally) *general* terms, either simple (like 'ball' and 'red') or complex (like 'red ball'). Depending on the *forms* of its premises and conclusion, a syllogism may be declared to be either *valid* or *invalid*, a valid syllogism being one whose conclusion follows necessarily from its premises, and hence one whose conclusion cannot fail to be true if its premises are true. An example of a valid syllogism would be 'All red balls are balls; all balls are round; therefore, all red balls are round.' An example of an invalid syllogism would be: 'Some red balls are round balls; some round balls are green; therefore, some red balls are green.' A system of syllogistic logic aims to tell us precisely which syllogisms are valid and which invalid simply by reference to the *forms* of their premises and conclusions (that is, without reference to the *meanings* of the general terms which they happen to contain). Thus, for example, the first syllogism just cited is valid because it has the form 'All *S* are *P*; all *P* are *Q*; therefore, all *S* are *Q*' – and any syllogism of this form must have a true conclusion if its premises are true.

Now Locke, we know, is no enemy to reason – by which he understands *demonstration* or *proof* – this being, according to him, one of our main sources of knowledge, especially in mathematical disciplines, such as geometry. Nor does he deny that it would be possible to dress up any chain of reasoning in syllogistic form, that is, to represent it as a series of syllogisms, with various steps in the chain recast as premises and conclusions in accordance with the formal rules of syllogistic logic. However, what he *does* deny is that we *in fact* employ syllogistic methods in following out a chain of demonstrative reasoning, and still more that we *should* employ them. As he implies, to suggest that the syllogistic method is the only right way to reason is to suppose, absurdly, that no one before Aristotle invented the method could reason properly at all (not even Aristotle himself!):

> God has not been so sparing to Men to make them barely two-legged Creatures, and left it to *Aristotle* to make them Rational.

> ... He has given them a Mind that can reason without being instructed in Methods of Syllogizing: The Understanding is not taught to reason by these Rules; it has a native Faculty to perceive the Coherence, or Incoherence of its *Ideas*, and can range them right, without any such perplexing Repetitions. (4.17.4)

Of course, philosophers and logicians today may feel that they have nothing to dispute with Locke about over this, since most of them are fairly contemptuous anyway of syllogistic methods. Today we are accustomed to learning instead the methods of formal logic first devised by Gottlob Frege and Bertrand Russell around the end of the nineteenth century – particularly the so-called predicate calculus, or first-order quantificational logic. Rather than representing a proposition like 'All round balls are green' as having the subject–predicate form 'All *RB* are *G*', Frege–Russell logic represents it as having the 'underlying' quantificational form 'For any x, if x is R and x is B, then x is G.' However, it is important to see that Locke's criticisms of syllogistic methods, portrayed as methods we allegedly either *do* or *should* employ in processes of demonstrative reasoning, apply equally to the modern formal methods of Frege and Russell, if they likewise are represented as either describing how we do, or prescribing how we should, reason deductively. For Locke's criticisms focus on the very issue of whether valid reasoning necessarily depends on or involves the identification of *formal* structures in premises and conclusions, and the application of *formal rules* in deriving the latter from the former.

Locke's position is that valid reasoning need depend on and involve *neither* of these. This is because he adopts what we may call a 'particularist' conception of valid argument, whereby the validity of an argument is solely determined by the meanings of the particular propositions which constitute its premises and conclusion, irrespective of any 'formal' characteristics those propositions may have in virtue of which the argument in question can be seen as exemplifying some *general pattern* of valid argument. Thus, on Locke's view, perceiving that a conclusion follows from given premises is a matter of intuitively grasping an immediate connection between the particular propositions in question, a connection in virtue of which one must be true if the others are, rather than a matter of seeing how those propositions possess such forms as render the argument in question an example of a valid argument form. (This 'particularism' appears to be connected in Locke's own mind – I think unnecessarily – with that brand of nominalism which we find in other parts of the *Essay*, and which in Chapter 7 (pp. 154, 162–3) I also called 'particularism': see, for example, *Essay*, 4.17.18.)

As I indicated earlier, this view of Locke's has contemporary relevance. There is much dispute amongst cognitive psychologists today over *how* human beings reason, one position being that we deploy what is called a 'mental logic' – that is, a system of formal rules of inference (supposedly of innate origin), not unlike those discovered by formal logicians over the centuries. Of course, to avoid the absurdity that I earlier reported Locke as having pointed out, advocates of 'mental logic' have to maintain that we deploy these formal rules quite *unconsciously*, since ordinary folk who are able to reason but have received no training in formal logic show no awareness of there being any such rules – not even the sort of awareness they show for the existence of rules of *grammar*. In opposition to the proponents of 'mental logic', other cognitive psychologists have proposed various alternative 'mechanisms' underlying our processes of inference: thus one school of thought contends that we deploy what it calls 'mental models' to check and certify the validity of arguments, while another contends that we exploit 'heuristics' – that is, rules of thumb which are not purely formal and topic-neutral, but geared to particular kinds of humanly encounterable situations (see Manktelow & Over 1990). However, none of these psychologists, oddly enough, has even begun to contemplate Locke's view of the nature of rational inference: that we *do not* deploy any quasi-mechanical system of 'rules' or 'models' in order to execute simple steps of rational inference – that we simply perceive the necessary connection between one proposition and another, without the mediation of any further cognitive apparatus. The human mind's capacity to reason validly may, rightly, strike us as marvellous (though not, I trust, as miraculous); but to attempt to reduce that capacity to something that can be executed by a mindless computer program, as the cognitive psychologists do, is not to dispel the mystery so much as to ignore the existence of the very phenomenon that needs to be explained (see further Lowe 1993).

Formal logical methods no doubt have their place, in mathematics and elsewhere, and Locke was perhaps excessively dismissive of their utility, but I am sure he was right to insist that we have a 'native Faculty to perceive the Coherence, or Incoherence of [our] *Ideas*' (4.17.4) which is partially constitutive of our rationality and without which, indeed, we should never have been able to construct formal systems of logic in the first place. There is, indeed, a peculiar absurdity in the proposal that our capacity to reason involves the unconscious implementation of just such formal systems as were, in fact, only *discovered* over many centuries through the painstaking exercise of that very capacity, by distinguished logicians from Aristotle to Frege.

As an afterthought, it is perhaps worth remarking that Locke's hostility to the claim that what he disparagingly calls 'magnified principles of demonstration', such as the laws of identity and non-contradiction, are *innate* (see Chapter 2) is partly a reflection of his scepticism about the degree to which such general logical principles actually *are* or *need to be* deployed in executing particular steps of demonstrative reasoning. Clearly, if we *do not* need to deploy such principles in order to reason demonstratively, there may, after all, be no grounds for supposing that we are equipped with a tacit knowledge of the principles even in early infancy. However, a resolution of this issue must await further research in both empirical psychology and logical theory.

The extent and limits of human knowledge

To what degree can Locke's conception of the scope of human understanding and knowledge be defended today? To a surprisingly large degree, I believe – surprising when one considers the very different world-views taken for granted in seventeenth- and in twentieth-century educated circles. Locke was writing at a time when it was implicitly believed even by the vast majority of enlightened thinkers that the world was only several thousand years old, that it had been created in a short period of time by a supremely powerful and intelligent Being, and that the Earth, though perhaps not at the centre of the universe, was in all probability the only inhabited region in a universe by no means inconceivably large by human standards. By contrast, almost all educated people today believe that the earth is a tiny, insignificant planet orbiting an insignificant star, that this star is just one of many millions in a galaxy which is itself only one amongst a vast number of others spread throughout a universe thousands of millions of years old and unimaginably huge in extent – a universe which appears to have developed in the way it has quite as much by chance as by law, from an initial 'singularity' involving stupendously high energies and temperatures but no very obvious trace of divine intervention. Human beings themselves are now thought to be the products of quite unpurposive processes of biological evolution, involving chance mutation and natural selection, rather than being the direct handiwork of God. Such 'native faculties' as human beings possess – such as a capacity to reason – cannot now be regarded as divine gifts designed to enable us to know and understand the world of our Creator, and hence cannot for that reason be assumed to be reliable and truth-revealing.

Why should genetic evolution have conferred upon us an ability to discern the true nature of the world of which we are a part? It would be facile to argue that we could not have survived as a species if we had been prone to form radically mistaken beliefs: first, because biological evolution does not guarantee that its products are *optimally* adapted to their environments, but at most that they are better adapted than their available competitors; and, second, because it is not obvious why false beliefs should not at least sometimes be conducive to the survival of those who possess them. And, after all, we *now* believe that our seventeenth-century predecessors *were* radically mistaken in their basic beliefs about the order and origin of natural phenomena, because their general world-view was, we now think, *quite wrong*. Evolutionary pressures might indeed eliminate a species prone to believe that poisonous plants are edible, but they can hardly be expected to have much bearing on the relative merits of beliefs about the age of the earth or the distance of the sun.

Now, however, we seem to be threatened by paradox: the modern scientific world-view, which leads us to regard our seventeenth-century forebears as radically mistaken in *their* world-view, is one which leads us also to regard *ourselves* as erratic products of unpurposive evolution, unblessed by any special faculty for revealing the true nature of our world – so what right do we have to our confidence in our own superior knowledge and understanding of nature? Such reflections may persuade us that Locke's humility regarding the scope of our 'real' knowledge was more justified than modern 'scientific' opinion would admit.

It may be helpful at this point to see if we can identify a solid core of commonsense belief about the 'external world' which is *stable*, in the sense of being relatively invulnerable to possible future revolutions in science as fundamental as those which have marked the transition from the seventeenth- to the twentieth-century world-view. Some radically relativist philosophers would no doubt contend that it is *impossible* to identify any such 'core' – a position which seems to commit them to an all-embracing anti-realism. Locke would, I am sure, resist such extreme scepticism and in the face of it defend what might be called a 'moderate' or 'modest' realism. Such a view holds that we can with complete confidence claim to know that an external world of causally interacting three-dimensional material objects exists, amidst which we ourselves are situated, our experience of those objects being a product of their interaction with us and affording us precisely that knowledge of their existence and behaviour as has just been claimed. This is a 'modest' realism in that it does not claim access to secure and unrevisable knowledge of what Locke calls the 'internal constitutions' or 'real essences' of physical things, allowing that, for instance, modern quantum physics may in time be discarded as emphatically as classical atomism has been today.

In my view, such a modest realism is probably the most that we can reasonably aspire to, so that I am broadly in agreement with what I take to be Locke's position. In earlier sections I did, it is true, point to the apparent *success* of modern science in probing the microstructure of the physical world as testifying to Locke's *excessive* modesty regarding the accessibility to us of the 'real essences' of physical things. But now I need to qualify those remarks rather than retract them. Locke was indeed – unsurprisingly and perfectly excusably – unaware of the degree to which the scientific investigation of nature might be facilitated by advances in technology and experimental method, and so could not have imagined how scientists would eventually devise techniques enabling them to test the empirical implications of different hypotheses concerning the atomic and molecular structure of matter. However, what still has to be acknowledged, despite the remarkable fruitfulness of such techniques, is that they still only leave us with *hypotheses*, however 'well confirmed' by experiment. One does not have to espouse Locke's perhaps unduly restrictive sense of the term 'knowledge' to contend that our being in possession of such well-confirmed hypotheses need not constitute *knowledge* of the microstructure of matter. (If one is an 'externalist' about knowledge, one may allow that it is *possible* that our current scientific beliefs constitute knowledge, while conceding that we cannot *know* that they do.) So I can consistently claim that Locke was excessively modest concerning the *practical* possibilities for extending the scope of scientific research, while agreeing with him on the more fundamental issue of the extent to which we can aspire to achieve a solid and unrevisable core of natural knowledge. With regard to the latter issue, Locke's modest realism does indeed seem to me to be a philosophically defensible position.

The version of 'modest' or 'moderate' realism that I should like to defend may be characterised as follows. First, it is an *empiricist* doctrine, in the sense that it grounds the 'core' of our natural knowledge in features of our perceptual experience. But the empiricism I have in mind is, unlike Locke's, *analytic* rather than *genetic*. By this I mean that it does not contend that we necessarily *acquire* our core of natural knowledge from our perceptual experience, whether by processes of deductive or probabilistic inference or by other, less 'rational' processes of any kind. It is perfectly possible that much of the core of our natural knowledge has an *innate* basis – perhaps explicable in evolutionary terms as being a cognitive inheritance which is conducive to our survival (though any such 'hypothesis' will not itself belong to the 'core'). Rather, the contention is that features of our perceptual experience serve to *justify* 'modest' realist knowledge-claims, and also that it is by reference to such features that the *content* of such claims is, at least in part, to be specified. In particular, I would maintain that, as Locke would put it, we have no 'positive idea' of many of the fundamental properties of natural objects (including, perhaps, ourselves), but only a 'relative idea' of them as being such properties as stand in certain *causal* and *logico-mathematical* (or 'structural') relations to qualitative features of our own perceptual experiences.

This still permits us to say quite a lot about the nature of the physical world – for instance, that it consists of three-dimensional objects moving about relative to one another and to ourselves. The structural organisation of our ongoing perceptual experience fully warrants, I would claim, a firm belief in the existence of such a world of objects as being causally implicated in the genesis of that experience. Alternative 'explanations' – such as Berkeley's idealist invocation of the immediate agency of God – are not so much rival 'hypotheses' as utterly idle speculations receiving no support whatever from features of experience itself. Berkeley's only hope is to attempt to unmask the modest realist's claim as being at bottom *unintelligible* – for instance, by appealing to his 'likeness principle', which forbids us to predicate univocally of 'external' objects anything predicable of features of perceptual experience ('an idea is like nothing but an idea'). But the modest realist may legitimately claim that there are 'topic-neutral' descriptions, notably *structural* descriptions definable in logico-mathematical terms, which are univocally applicable *both* to features of experience *and* to features of the physical world.

Geometrical descriptions provide the most obvious example of these. For instance, the qualitative features of visual experience exhibit a two-dimensional or surface-like geometrical structure, variations in which over time almost always warrant a description of that structure as being, formally speaking, a 'projection' of a three-dimensional space of moving objects possessing relatively stable three-dimensional forms. Although this fact is, of course, readily explicable by reference to physical optics and the physiology of human vision, such an explanation does not itself belong to the 'core' of our natural knowledge. By contrast, the sort of projective description in question is one whose applicability *can* be discerned purely by noticing the geometrical organisation of one's visual experience as it varies over time, without appeal to any putative facts about the structure of the human eye and the behaviour of light. However, it would apparently involve an utterly miraculous series of coincidences for our visual experience to exhibit this systematically projective character if there were *not* in fact a *real* world of objects actually standing in appropriate projective relationships to our visual experience and causally implicated in its production.

But observe that the most that this consideration entitles us to say about the *nature* of those 'external' objects concerns their *geometrical* form and relationships over time, statable in the same sort of logico-mathematical terms as are used to describe the geometrical structure of visual experience itself. (This is not, of course, to say that visual experience and its objects share exactly the *same* geometrical structure – that they are exactly *isomorphic* – since they are, as we have seen, related only *projectively*, the former constituting a two-dimensional projection of the latter: but it is still the same *geometrical* language that is used to describe both in stating them to be related in this way.) Thus, whereas in the case of visual experience we are aware not only of its formal, geometrical structure but also of its 'matter' – its variegated phenomenal *colour-content* – in the case of the *objects* of that experience, the experience provides us with knowledge of their *formal* structure alone, telling us nothing about their 'matter', that is, about what it is that 'fills out' their spatial form. It is in this sense that Locke was right to speak of physical matter as being, ultimately, 'something we know not what'. (Even *solidity*, understood as a propensity in objects to resist penetration or deformation, is something we apparently only understand by reference to its effects as manifested to us by alterations in the *shapes* and *motions* of objects, and thus in logico-mathematical terms; what 'real quality' in objects, if any, is the ground of this propensity may perhaps be a matter for legitimate scientific speculation, but is not something an understanding of which can be regarded as being part of our 'core' of natural knowledge.)

One apparent difficulty facing 'modest' realism of the type just outlined concerns the place within that scheme of our understanding of *causation*, both between natural objects and between them and ourselves. Modest realism not only posits a world of three-dimensional objects moving in space, but also posits *causal* relationships between them and our experience, precisely in order to *explain* the systematic structural co-variations between experience and its objects, as illustrated earlier in the visual case. But, as Hume was to urge, there seems to be a problem in understanding what we could *mean* by attributing causal powers to natural objects. This, however, was because Hume could not permit himself to accept Locke's contention that our basic concept of causation is grounded in our experience of *our own power of agency*, when we exercise our will in performing any action. According to Locke:

> The *Idea* of the beginning of motion, we have only from reflection on what passes in our selves, where we find by Experience, that barely by willing it, barely by a thought of the Mind, we can move the parts of our Bodies, which were before at rest. (2.21.4)

Hume held that we have no more insight into *our own* putative causal powers than we do into those of natural objects, and hence cannot use such insight to help us to grasp what it means to posit causal relations between natural objects (see Hume 1978, pp. 632–3). But in this I believe he was mistaken, because I think it is simply incoherent to suppose, as he does, that we just learn, by repeated experience, that our volitions tend to be followed by events realising the intentional contents of those volitions – for instance, that I just learn by repeated experience that a volition of mine to raise my arm is regularly succeeded by a perception of my arm's rising. Rather, volition has to be conceived, as Locke conceived it, as involving an experience of real agency (even if circumstances should on occasion conspire to frustrate the success of that agency) – thus providing us with an 'idea' of causal power.

If that is correct, then I believe that we do indeed have the conceptual resources to grasp what it means to attribute causal power to other things, including natural objects. We do not have to think of those objects as being *intelligent* agents like ourselves, capable of engaging in *voluntary* action (as Berkeley would complain, in objecting to the whole notion of unthinking matter), since the claim is *not* that our basic conception of causation is framed in terms of volition, but rather that our conception of volition – which is fully adequate itself – incorporates an ineliminable causal component, a notion of 'bringing-about', which is capable of being unambiguously transferred to cases *not* involving volition.

The claims that I have been making on behalf of 'modest' realism – claims which I believe are broadly Lockean in spirit – are admittedly very sketchy and quite controversial. This is not the place for me to develop and defend them in detail. But I hope I have said enough to give some indication as to how a modern follower of Locke could hope to defend a set of doctrines, recognisably akin to his own brand of moderate empiricist realism, which allows us to possess a *real* but *limited* knowledge and understanding of the natural world – an understanding which nonetheless has, quite arguably, 'all the real conformity it can, or ought to have, with Things without us' (4.4.4).

Bibliography

The standard modern edition of Locke's *Essay* is the Clarendon Edition, edited by Peter H. Nidditch (Oxford: Clarendon Press, 1975). This is based on the fourth edition of 1700. The Clarendon Edition of Locke's *Works* includes many volumes of his letters. A good modern biography of Locke is Maurice Cranston's *John Locke: A Biography* (London: Longman, 1957). There are many modern studies of Locke's philosophy – notably Mackie 1976, Woolhouse 1983 and Alexander 1985 – but the most important in recent years is undoubtedly Michael Ayers's two-volume work (Ayers 1991). The doyen of modern Locke scholars is John Yolton: see, in particular, Yolton 1970. Two good collections of articles are Tipton (ed.) 1977 and Chappell (ed.) 1994. A very useful bibliographical guide to work on Locke is Roland Hall and Roger Woolhouse's *Eighty Years of Locke Scholarship* (Edinburgh: Edinburgh University Press, 1983). More recent publications are listed annually in *The Locke Newsletter*, edited by Roland Hall, which also contains many interesting articles and reviews.

Aaron, R. I. 1937: *John Locke* (London: Oxford University Press), 3rd edn 1971.

Alexander, P. 1985: *Ideas, Qualities and Corpuscles* (Cambridge University Press).

Alston, W. & Bennett, J. 1988: 'Locke on People and Substances', *Philosophical Review* 97, pp. 25–46.

Aristotle 1963: *Categories and De Interpretatione*, trans. J. L. Ackrill (Oxford: Clarendon Press).

Ashworth, E. J. 1984: 'Locke on Language', *Canadian Journal of Philosophy* 14, pp. 45–73.

Ayers, M. R. 1991: *Locke* (London: Routledge).

Bechtel, W. & Abrahamsen, A. 1991: *Connectionism and the Mind* (Oxford: Blackwell).

Bennett, J. 1987: 'Substratum', *History of Philosophy Quarterly* 4, pp. 197–215.

Berkeley, G. 1975: *Philosophical Works*, ed. M. R. Ayers (London: Dent).

Block, N. (ed.) 1981: *Imagery* (Cambridge, Mass.: MIT Press).

Bower, T. G. R. 1989: *The Rational Infant* (New York: Freeman).

Boyle, R. 1666: 'Origin of Forms and Qualities', in M. A. Stewart (ed.), *Selected Philosophical Papers of Robert Boyle* (Manchester: Manchester University Press, 1979).

Butler, J. 1736: 'Of Personal Identity', in J. Perry (ed.), *Personal Identity* (Berkeley & Los Angeles: University of California Press).

Chappell, V. 1989: 'Locke and Relative Identity,' *History of Philosophy Quarterly* 6, pp. 69–83.

—— (ed.) 1994: *The Cambridge Companion to Locke* (Cambridge: Cambridge University Press).

Chomsky, N. 1972: *Language and Mind* (New York: Harcourt, Brace, Jovanovich).

Copenhaver, B. P. & Schmitt, C. B. 1992: *Renaissance Philosophy* (Oxford: Oxford University Press).

Dancy, J. 1985: *Introduction to Contemporary Epistemology* (Oxford: Basil Blackwell).

Descartes, R. 1984: *The Philosophical Writings of Descartes*, ed. J. Cottingham, R. Stoothoof & D. Murdoch (Cambridge: Cambridge University Press).

Dummett, M. 1981: *Frege: Philosophy of Language*, 2nd edn (London: Duckworth).

Fodor, J. A. 1976: *The Language of Thought* (Hassocks: Harvester Press).

—— 1981: 'The Present Status of the Innateness Controversy', in his *Representations* (Brighton: Harvester Press).

—— 1990: *A Theory of Content and Other Essays* (Cambridge, Mass.: MIT Press).

Frankfurt, H. G. 1982: 'Freedom of the Will and the Concept of a Person', in
  G. Watson (ed.), *Free Will* (Oxford: Oxford University Press).
Galileo 1954: *Dialogues Concerning Two New Sciences* (1638), trans. H.
  Crew & A. de Salvio (New York: Dover).
Geach, P. T. 1980: *Reference and Generality*, 3rd edn (Ithaca, NY: Cornell
  University Press).
Hacking, I. 1975: *Why Does Language Matter to Philosophy?* (Cambridge:
  Cambridge University Press).
Hardin, C. L. 1988: *Color for Philosophers* (Indianapolis, Ind.: Hackett).
Hume, D. 1978: *Treatise of Human Nature* (1739–40), ed. L. A. Selby-Bigge
  & P. H. Nidditch (Oxford: Clarendon Press).
Jackson, F. 1977: *Perception: A Representative Theory* (Cambridge:
  Cambridge University Press).
James, W. 1890: *Principles of Psychology* (New York: Henry Holt).
Kant, I. 1929: *Critique of Pure Reason* (1787), trans. N. Kemp Smith (London:
  Macmillan).
Lakoff, G. 1987: *Women, Fire and Dangerous Things* (Chicago, Ill.:
  University of Chicago Press).
Leibniz, G. W. 1981: *New Essays on Human Understanding*, trans. P. Remnant
  & J. Bennett (Cambridge: Cambridge University Press).
Locke, J. 1967: *Two Treatises of Government*, ed. P. Laslett, 2nd edn
  (Cambridge: Cambridge University Press).
Lowe, E. J. 1986: 'Necessity and the Will in Locke's Theory of Action',
  History of Philosophy Quarterly 3, pp. 149–63.
—— 1989a: 'What is a Criterion of Identity?', *Philosophical Quarterly* 39,
  pp. 1–21.
—— 1989b: *Kinds of Being* (Oxford: Basil Blackwell).
—— 1991a: 'Substance and Selfhood', *Philosophy* 66, pp. 81–99.
—— 1991b: 'Real Selves: Persons as a Substantial Kind', in D. Cockburn
  (ed.), *Human Beings* (Cambridge: Cambridge University Press).
—— 1992: 'Experience and its Objects', in T. Crane (ed.), *The Contents of
  Experience* (Cambridge: Cambridge University Press).
—— 1993: 'Rationality, Deduction and Mental Models', in K. I. Manktelow
  & D. E. Over (eds), *Rationality* (London: Routledge).
McCann, H. 1974: 'Volition and Basic Action', *Philosophical Review* 83, pp.
  451–73.
Mackie, J. L. 1976: *Problems from Locke* (Oxford: Clarendon Press).
Manktelow, K. I. & Over, D. E. 1990: *Inference and Understanding* (London:
  Routledge).
Melden, A. I. 1961: *Free Action* (London: Routledge & Kegan Paul).

Morgan, M. J. 1977: *Molyneux's Question* (Cambridge: Cambridge University Press).

Nagel, T. 1979: 'What is it Like to be a Bat?' and 'Subjective and Objective', in his *Mortal Questions* (Cambridge: Cambridge University Press).

Newton, I. 1686: 'Rules of Reasoning in Philosophy', in Book III of his *Principia*, trans. A. Motte & F. Cajori (Berkeley & Los Angeles: University of California Press, 1934).

Noonan, H. W. 1989: *Personal Identity* (London: Routledge).

Parfit, D. 1984: *Reasons and Persons* (Oxford: Clarendon Press).

Perry, J. (ed.) 1975: *Personal Identity* (Berkeley & Los Angeles: University of California Press).

Popper, K. R. & Eccles, J. C. 1977: *The Self and its Brain* (Berlin: Springer).

Putnam, H. 1975: 'The Meaning of "Meaning"', in his *Mind, Language and Reality* (Cambridge: Cambridge University Press).

Quine, W. V. 1960: *Word and Object* (Cambridge, Mass.: MIT Press).

Reid, T. 1785: 'Of Mr Locke's Account of Personal Identity', in J. Perry (ed.), *Personal Identity* (Berkeley & Los Angeles: University of California Press).

Russell, B. 1959a: *The Problems of Philosophy* (1912) (London: Oxford University Press).

—— 1959b: *My Philosophical Development* (London: George Allen & Unwin).

Ryle, G. 1949: *The Concept of Mind* (London: Hutchinson).

Searle, J. R. 1983: *Intentionality* (Cambridge: Cambridge University Press).

Strawson, P. F. 1959: *Individuals* (London: Methuen).

Tipton, I. C. (ed.) 1977: *Locke on Human Understanding* (Oxford: Oxford University Press).

Tye, M. 1989: *The Metaphysics of Mind* (Cambridge: Cambridge University Press).

Wiggins, D. 1980: *Sameness and Substance* (Oxford: Basil Blackwell).

Williams, B. 1973: 'Deciding to Believe', in his *Problems of the Self* (Cambridge: Cambridge University Press).

Wittgenstein, L. 1953: *Philosophical Investigations* (Oxford: Basil Blackwell).

Woolhouse, R. S. 1983: *Locke* (Brighton: Harvester Press).

Yolton, J. W. 1970: *Locke and the Compass of Human Understanding* (Cambridge: Cambridge University Press).

Index